NATHAN DRISKELL

Is Your Child Addicted To Electronics?

30 Days of Healing and Recovery for your Child and Family

First edition

ISBN: 9781521552216

This book was professionally typeset on Reedsy.
Find out more at reedsy.com

Contents

INTRODUCTION

I t's the same old story. It's dinner time, and John is in his room, playing his Xbox. You have yelled over and over for him to come down, with no result. He yells he is in the middle of a game and cannot stop. You wait 5-10-15 minutes, while dinner grows cold. You begin to eat, annoyed, and frustrated. The same thing happens every night. He never comes to the table when called. He rarely does homework on his own. He is always playing games or watching YouTube videos. He yells at you often and does not understand why you are upset.

You have grounded him from electronics before. When you have hidden the Xbox, he finds it and plays anyway. You have taken away his tablet, which he then steals your phone. He yells and screams at you for not allowing him to get online. He says all his friends are online, and they don't have a mean parent like you.

A week passes. You get your credit card bill and discover $200 of charges you did not authorize. You find it is for games from the Xbox Store, and figure out John stole your credit card to buy them. You feel so angry, so betrayed, and you don't know what to do anymore. Nothing works. Now John is a thief, and when you confront him, he then turns it back on you. He yells other parents buy their kids' games, and that without games, he cannot play with his friends and cannot have a life.

Does this sound familiar? For many parents, this is a typical scenario. Most kids now spend eight hours a day or more on electronics, even on school days. Most of their hobbies are online, not to mention their friends. Combine social interactions with hobbies such as playing games and watching videos, and most of their free time is online.

The question is, if you have a child like John, what do you do? You cannot ban electronics until they are 18 years old, as they need them for school, work, and social interaction. You had likely talked to them before, which they ignored. You are out of options and do not know how to help your child balance electronics with life.

The scenario above, or something similar, is likely why you purchased this book. You feel tired, hopeless, and want this to change. To help, I have created a 30-day plan to help you better communicate with your child while beginning to battle their addiction to electronics. Each day will consist of at least one activity I want you to complete. Some activities will be with your child; others will be for you. Much will change in the next month, as you will be learning more about your child, his or her addiction, and the role you play in it.

Introductions are in order. My name is Nathan Driskell, and I am a therapist in the Houston area. I specialize in treating Internet Addiction, as I am an Internet addict. I spent six years playing an online game for 10-12 hours a day while I was in college. I continue to struggle with addiction issues even though I quit the game many years ago. I have found for me; addiction is an everyday struggle I have to fight. The days I have clear, precise goals are the days I do well. Days I am not focused, or mentally tired, are the days I stumble. Unlike drugs or alcohol, abstaining from the Internet is impossible. The temptation is always there to play a game, or watch a video, instead of doing work or other activities. If I, an adult who is a therapist, struggle with this addiction, imagine how a child feels? After working with over 300 children who are Internet addicts, I have found most have issues beyond their addiction to electronics. Without addressing these issues, the addiction persists.

In this book, I will incorporate techniques and activities I use with many of my children and adolescent clients who are addicted to the Internet. Some of these activities will be quick and easy to complete. Others will take time and effort to begin and finish. While working this book, try to complete all activities to build toward a final product. If you cannot finish an activity within a day, continue until it is complete. Once done, proceed with the book. Life sometimes gets in the way, and you need to be flexible.

In addition to completing this book, I recommend working with a therapist who understands addiction, especially Internet and electronics addiction. This book is NOT a substitute for therapy! Working through this book with a qualified therapist will produce the maximum effect.

In the first part of the book, you will begin learning about your child's addiction, what they gain from the addiction, and how you influence it. Insight into your child's addiction will help you learn more about your child and how to better communicate with them. You will be asked to evaluate yourself as well, as your well-being affects your child. You will be monitoring your child's time online and learn more about their online activities.

In the second part of this book, you will begin to change how your child interacts with electronics. You will limit their access to games, videos, and electronics while introducing them to alternatives. You will NOT be removing all access to electronics, as your child needs to learn how to live with them. At times, these steps will be difficult to complete, and your child will resist.

In the final section of this book, you will establish long-term rules regarding online access and begin to plan for your child's future. You will review the techniques you learned in this book and will learn to communicate better with your child going forward.

I warn you; this book will be difficult to complete, as there is much to do, and you will experience increased conflict and tension in the home. Change is difficult, especially for a parent who is having problems with their child. You, as a parent, will have to make these changes and enforce them. Some days you will be tired and will feel like giving up. If you feel the need, take a break for a day or two, then come back. Once you have completed this book, you will have a greater understanding of your child, their addiction, and how you can help balance electronics with real life.

PART 1: INSIGHT

DAY 1: YOUR FAMILY

Beginning to tackle your child's addiction is no easy task. You have been trying for some time to help your child balance life with screens. You have likely had many arguments, often with yelling and screaming from your child. Children today do not see their screen time as a problem because they have always had online access. With their friends spending 8+ hours online a day, they see their online time as normal. As a parent, you likely have a hard time seeing their viewpoint, and vice versa.

Over time, your family's relationship has suffered. Stress from your child's addiction is taking a toll on the household and all individuals within. On most nights, are the members of your family isolated in their rooms? When was the last time you have had a meal with all the members of your family? When was the last time your family went out and did something fun together?

Your family, as a unit, is breaking. You have probably seen this and have tried to force it back together. Instead of helping, you cause more division and conflict. One of this book's goals is to improve communication with your child and family as a whole. To put your family back together, you first need to focus on each member's recent accomplishments and challenges. What has each member done well lately? What challenges do they face? What have you done, as a parent, to encourage these accomplishments and help manage the challenges? A complete picture of each family member will help you build a realistic picture, which will open up lines of communication.

Accomplishments

It is human nature to focus more on problems than success. Over time, accomplishments are minimized, becoming expected. If your child has made good grades for years, it becomes expected they will continue to make good grades. Even though children should become self-motivated as they age, they still require praise. If accomplishments are not acknowledged, motivation will decrease.

Right now, it may be difficult to notice your child's accomplishments, given the magnitude of their problems. You may be too caught up in everything wrong to see what is right. The more you complain or yell at your child about their screen time, the more they learn to tune you out. It would help if you spoke to them about something they are interested in to gain their attention.

One of the first changes you will make is how you communicate with your child. You will no longer yell at them and only focus on their failures. You are going to work to talk in level tones and to discuss topics beyond their addiction. Talking about their interests, even if they are online, will help grab their attention.

Challenges

Every member of your family has challenges, including yourself. Sometimes your family needs help in overcoming these challenges. Other times, they need to find solutions themselves. Knowing more about these challenges gives insight into their world.

Think of each member of your family, and consider the challenges they are currently facing. If you have a child who is a teenager, think about some of the problems a teenager would face today. Sometimes, communication is with actions, not words. When one member of the family is an addict, it is common to ignore the other members. Family members ignored may find ways to voice their frustrations by creating problems needing your attention. Focus on all members of your family, adults included, and think about their current challenges.

Parents: The Agent of Change

As a parent, you are responsible for the physical and mental health of your family. What happens then if you are not at your best? Your health and well-being are more important than your children's, as if you suffer, they will as well.

If your family is to change, you are the one responsible for it. In therapeutic terms, this is called the "agent of change." An agent of change is the primary force that creates and promotes change in a family system. Without this agent, change rarely occurs. Therefore, the agent of change needs to be in good health, both mentally and physically.

To that end, how have you been doing lately? How is your mental health? How are your stress levels? Are there any physical problems affecting you? If so, what are you doing about them? How is your diet? How much sleep are you getting? Do you have any addictions yourself?

To battle your child's addiction to electronics, much of how you think and act needs to change. At times, these changes will be difficult and taxing. From now on, you need to improve your mental and physical health so that you can be a model for your child. Later in this book, you will make adjustments to your routine and learn how to battle negative thoughts.

Today's Activities

Today, you will make a list of the accomplishments and challenges for each member of your family, including parents. Items on your list need to be recent, within the past six months. The list can look like the following example:

Tommy
Accomplishments:

- Made a B on his algebra test.
- Mowed the lawn last week.
- Went out with a friend, instead of binging on video games in his room.
- Helped make dinner last night.

Challenges:

- Binged 10 hours on the Xbox yesterday.
- Keeps his phone out during dinner, even if told to put it away.
- Yelled at me when told to come to dinner.
- Made a D on his history assignment.

Try to include at least four items for accomplishments and challenges. Make sure the list is for all family members, including yourself. Be honest, even if your challenges are difficult to admit. While making this list, try to include both parents, if possible. You do not need to share this list with your children unless you think it would be beneficial.

The purpose of this list is to see the positives of your family, including members who sometimes slip beneath the cracks. Learning to see positives in a sea of negatives will encourage you to continue. When you talk with your children, congratulate them on their accomplishments while helping them with their challenges.

Quick To-Do List

1. Create a list of accomplishments and challenges for all family members.

Tomorrow's Focus

To begin making changes in your family, you will first need to step back and change yourself. Tomorrow, you will start a self-analysis to determine what changes you need to make in your life. You will take the list you've done for yourself and expand it, focusing more on yourself, your struggles, and your outlook. You will need to be honest with yourself, as you will need to admit any addictions or struggles you face. Tomorrow may be the most stressful day of the book, as it has little to do with your child, but you. Complete your list, and be prepared to evaluate yourself tomorrow.

DAY 2: YOURSELF

O n Day 1, we discussed improving your communication with your family by focusing on their accomplishments, as well as their challenges. Today, we will shift the focus from your family to you. You are just as important as your children; more so, in fact. As their agent of change, it is up to you to manage their future.

To that end, an honest evaluation of yourself is needed. Get out the list you made of your accomplishments and challenges, as you will need it today.

Your Accomplishments

What accomplishments did you put on your list? Sometimes, it's hard to know what qualifies. Sometimes, paying the bills on time can feel like a major accomplishment. What have you done right in raising your children? Are you keeping track of their grades? Are they on track for their doctor's appointments? When your kids come to you for help, do you listen?

For these accomplishments, feel good about them. Just because they are a required part of parenting does not mean you cannot take enjoyment in them. Beyond parenting duties, what success have you had at work? What has gone well in your relationships? Accomplishments come in many forms; for each, give yourself credit. For your accomplishments, what can you do to repeat them?

Your Challenges

What issues are you going through right now? Guaranteed to be on your list is your child's addiction to electronics. Most likely, your child's grades and social relationships are as well. Beyond these, what other challenges are you facing? If you have other children, how are they dealing with the stress of your child's addiction? Are you under extreme stress?

How is your relationship with your spouse? If you are married or are in a relationship, how is the addiction affecting it? Are there arguments on how to deal with the addiction? Addiction is one of the leading causes of breakups in relationships, regardless of who is addicted.

Has your work been affected by your child's addiction? How about your focus and attention? How about your personal life? When was the last time you did something fun for you? For you to combat these challenges, you need to be aware of them.

Your Addictions

Now comes the tricky part. Do you have any addictions? Some examples include work, sugar, social media, games, sports, pornography, alcohol, and drugs. Addiction is common for most people, as it is easy to become dependent on a chemical or activity.

The goal is not to shame you, but to be honest about yourself and your problems. When someone is addicted, changes can be seen by others. As you have noticed changes with your child, he or she may have noticed changes in you. If your child feels you have an addiction, they will use your addiction as an excuse to continue theirs.

It is vital to work on your addictions and be honest about them. If you feel your child is aware of your addiction, you need to discuss your addiction with your child. You are not encouraging addiction by discussing it. Quite the opposite, you are taking responsibility. In battling your addiction, you will be a model for your child, which will help them fight theirs.

If you feel you do not have an addiction, step back, and see if your actions could look addictive to your child. After an honest evaluation, you will likely find things you need to change in your life.

Your Health

How is your health lately? Are you sleeping at night? Are you eating well? What coping skills, if any, are you using to manage life's stresses? Having a proper diet, sleeping well, and managing stress are important for you and your child.

If you have any mental health conditions, what are you doing to manage them? Are you taking your medications? Are you seeing a therapist? If so, are you listening to your therapist and completing their assignments? Anxiety and depression are common conditions that can affect anyone. If you have felt depressed or suffer from high anxiety levels, see a therapist or psychiatrist for assessment. Do not let stigma or pride get in the way. Feeling depressed or suffering from extreme levels of stress is NOT normal. Getting professional help can be one of the most important steps you take.

If you have any physical conditions, how do they affect your daily life? Are they taking up time in your day, or do they cause excessive stress? Pain is a common condition for many that can affect mood. It is easy to become upset and yell at your children while in pain. If you are dealing with pain, you need to make a plan on how to manage it.

Today's Activity

Today, you will take the list you made yesterday with your accomplishments and challenges, and expand on them. Put more detail into the accomplishments you have had as of late. Make sure to include your abilities as a parent, your work life, and your social life.

For the challenges you are going to expand on them by writing down strategies to tackle them. Below is an example:

Challenge: Feeling overworked at home.
Strategy: Create a schedule to add time for relaxation, with two days per month for relaxation with no work.

Challenge: Not getting enough sleep.
Strategy: Make sure to go to bed at the same time each night. Do an activity before bed to tire me out.

Challenge: Feeling anxious all the time.
Strategy: See a psychiatrist or therapist about my anxiety.

Make sure your list is realistic and attainable. It is not realistic to have no anxiety or to have perfect sleep. For the rest of this book, you are going to enact these strategies in your life. These are changes you will make over the next 30 days to improve your life and your health. If you have any addictions, they take priority over all other problems. To build trust with your family, you will need to battle these addictions head-on.

Quick To-Do List

1. Expand on your list's accomplishments and challenges. Add strategies to each item on your list. Pay particular attention to any addictions you may have and how to plan to tackle them.

2. Prepare to use these strategies for the rest of the book, so you are better equipped physically and mentally.

Tomorrow's Focus

Today was a stressful day. You may feel angry, tired, or drained. You may feel like today was a waste of time, that your focus should be on your child, not you. These feelings are common. However, you need to be at your best if you hope to improve your child's life. Tomorrow, your focus turns to your family. Tomorrow, you will have a family meeting, where you will sit down and talk about the family's problems and how each member can use their strengths to combat these problems.

DAY 3: THE FAMILY MEETING

Today, you are going to do something you most likely have never done. You will gather your family together and have a meeting about their accomplishments, challenges, and your family's overall direction. Your children are going to think this is strange, weird, and may resist attending. You will discuss your concerns over your children's screen time and discuss any challenges you face.

Preparation

To prepare for this meeting, you will need the list of accomplishments and challenges you made for all family members on Day 1. Look over this list and make any updates you have noticed over the past two days. You are going to use this list as the basis for the meeting. You will be addressing each member of the family, discussing their accomplishments, strengths, and challenges over the past six months.

Accomplishments

At the beginning of the meeting, you will discuss its purpose; to bring the family closer together by opening communication. You will then discuss the accomplishments each family member has had over the past six months. Accomplishments do not need to be grand; sometimes, basic tasks qualify. Ask each member to discuss any accomplishments you may have missed, so they have a voice in the discussion.

Each parent needs to discuss their accomplishments and what they have done to help the family over the past six months. Do not spend too much time discussing your accomplishments, as your children may tune out of you do.

Strengths

Next, ask each member of the family to discuss their current strengths. Expect your children to be uncomfortable during much of the meeting, as they are not accustomed to having these types of discussions. Encourage each of your children to speak about their strengths while limiting negative comments from others. By beginning the meeting with accomplishments and strengths, your children may not see the meeting as a punishment.

Challenges

Next, you will discuss the challenges you see within the family. Start this section with your challenges. Be honest with them, as much as you can with your children. For example, challenges in your work, health, or any addictions you may have. Do not blame anyone for these challenges, especially your children. Blame and shame will only distance you from them. Be honest with any struggles you have had, and ask your children for suggestions on how to solve some of these problems.

Next, ask each member of the family any challenges they have had recently. Let them begin the process by talking about problems from their viewpoint. They may mention problems you have not noticed. For each problem, ask them how they plan to solve them and provide suggestions if needed. Ensure each child has input in how they will solve their problems to take ownership of them. If you have noticed problems your child does not bring up, discuss them, and ask your child how they plan to solve them.

Wrap-Up

Towards the end of the meeting, ask the family about activities they would like to do together soon. Ask them if there is something they wish to do or someplace to go. Focus on something fun and different, something that may not involve electronics. As you work this book, you will be making Family Days, where your family goes and does something fun as a group. At the end of this meeting, get ideas from your family, and begin to plan.

What If the Meeting Fails?

The meeting may not go well, depending on your children and how they respond. Some may refuse to attend and may insult you for asking. Others may get up and walk out as you begin discussing challenges. Others may not pay attention and make sarcastic remarks. What do you do if this happens?

First, you need to expect resistance. Your family has likely not done this before. On the surface, it may sound silly and cliché. Expect to have problems, and you will be mentally able to handle setbacks.

If a member of your family refuses to attend the meeting, have it anyway. Invite them to the meeting, and if they refuse, talk to them alone about the purpose of the meeting. There could be many reasons why they do not want to attend, such as anxiety or resistance to change. If one of your children refuses to participate, do not get upset or raise your voice. Discuss with your child in private instead.

Sometimes, it is the spouse or other parent who refuses to attend. If this happens, have the meeting anyway. Parents, at times, can be just as stubborn as kids. Discuss the purpose of the meeting with the other parent, focusing on communication. If they refuse to attend, hold the meeting anyway, and discuss the meeting's outcome in private.

A Learning Opportunity

No matter the outcome of the meeting, you will learn more about your family and yourself. Note how each member responds to the other and what they say. Hopefully, you can learn more about your children and their problems. In any event, you will find out how much they are willing to communicate. If your children do not talk much in the meeting, talk to them in private afterward.

It will take time for your family to improve. One meeting will not dramatically change your family. This meeting is the beginning of open communication with your family. At times, it will be rough. Mediate these exchanges, and be human with your children. Asking them for help could go a long way to repairing relationships within your family.

Today's Activity

Go ahead and schedule the family meeting. Try to find a time when each person is available. You may need to schedule this meeting for another day or on the weekend. Tell your children that you want to have a meeting and ask them for help. They may appear confused or perplexed, which is ok. Do not tell them that the family meeting will be about their problems, as they may refuse to attend. How you sell the meeting is important. The meeting's goal is for each member of the family to have a voice so that each one can communicate their accomplishments and challenges.

If you cannot have the family meeting tonight, wait to continue this book until it is complete. Information learned at the meeting is needed for the rest of the book. Until the family meeting, focus on your health while working to solve the problems you identified yesterday.

Quick To-Do List

1. Schedule a family meeting with all members. In the meeting, focus on each member's accomplishments, strengths, and challenges. If the meeting is days in the future, delay continuing this book until then, instead focus on the problems you identified yesterday.

Tomorrow's Focus

Once the family meeting is complete, you will begin to learn how much time your child spends online and the activities they perform. Over the next four days, you will start monitoring their time online, learning how much time they spend. Through this process, you will learn more about the applications or games they use, and later, the reasons behind their use. For much of the next week, you will gather information on your child's addiction and begin to learn what they gain from it. Once you have collected this information, you will begin creating a plan to combat their addiction, helping them find a balance between electronics and life.

DAY 4: DIGITAL FOOTPRINT, PART 1 - ACCESS

H ow did the family meeting go? Was it productive? Did you learn anything new about your family, especially your child that is addicted to electronics? Did they bring up their addiction, or did you? Hopefully, you learned something last night and began to open up lines of communication within your family.

The next four days will focus on your child's online habits, with the first focusing on the devices he or she uses to connect to the Internet. You are going to make a list of all devices, from cell phones to tablets to computers.

Access = Gateway Drug

Knowing what electronics your child uses to access the Internet is critical, as you will make changes to how your child uses these devices.

Most people use many different electronic devices to access the Internet. It can be gaming consoles such as the Playstation 4, the Xbox One, or the Nintendo Switch. It may be tablets, such as iPads or Samsung Tabs. It could be Portable gaming consoles such as the Nintendo DS. It could be the Oculus Rift or the HTC Vive, big names in virtual reality technology for PC.

In the days to follow, you will be tracking how much time your child spends online on each device, as well as what activities they conduct. You are going to make a digital snapshot of their online life. You will begin to see just how much time they spend online, as well as their activities. Creating a digital footprint sounds simple, but in reality, it is not. The next few days will take work on your part, as you're going to keep a logbook of your child's online activities.

Today's Activity

You are going to make a list of every device your child uses to access the Internet. You will then rank the devices in order of most use. Be thorough and think about how your child accesses the Internet. Do they use a friend's DS? Do they borrow their sister's iPad? The devices at the top of your list will be the ones you will need to pay particular attention to as you work through this book.

Quick To-Do List

1. Make a list of all devices your child uses online and order them from the greatest usage.

Tomorrow's Focus

With the list complete, you will begin to monitor your child's Internet usage. In the next two days, you will record all their time online. Do not ask your child to deviate from their normal routine, as you need to see an accurate picture. Once you have a complete picture of their online usage, you will begin to see how much their addiction affects their lives and yours. Continue taking care of yourself by looking over your list of challenges you made on Day 2.

DAY 5 & 6: DIGITAL FOOTPRINT, PART 2 – CATALOGING

I t is time to begin cataloging your child's time online. For the next two days, you are going to note everything they do online. Examples include chatting with friends, playing games, and watching videos. You will record all time spent on non-work or school activities. While it will not be possible to record time outside the home, you will do your best to estimate their online usage.

The question is, how will you record all their time online? You have two options. You can carry a logbook and manually record their time, which will prove difficult. Or you can use an application for your smartphone, tablet, or computer to aid in the process.

No matter what you choose, you will need to manually record some of your child's online activities. No one program will record all online time across all devices. Being as thorough as possible is the goal, so you can see a realistic picture of how much time your child spends with electronics.

If you have an Android phone or have a PC, Mac, or Linux system, the best program to use is called RescueTime. If you have an iPhone or any device that uses iOS, you can track how much time you spend on applications via system settings.

What is RescueTime?

RescueTime is an application that sits in the background of your phone or PC that collects data on the programs you use. It sets timers for each application or website. It logs how much time spent and then puts this information in an easy to use graph format. For example, if you are using Twitter on your PC, it would log how much time you spend on it each day and any other websites or applications used.

The great thing about RescueTime is the lack of user interaction. You do not need to start and stop timers, like other timing applications. You can install the program, set it up, then go about your day without having to remember to start or stop a timer.

Not only does RescueTime collect data, but you can also set goals and even tell it to limit your access to certain websites or applications. For example, you can tell RescueTime to restrict access to social media apps like Facebook or Snapchat, and it will not permit access until you allow it.

If you have a PC, Mac, Android Phone, or Linux OS, then install RescueTime on all devices your child uses. For this book, we will assume you have installed RescueTime, as you will use it beyond this chapter. I recommend the Premium version, which will give you a 14-day free trial. This version is $6.00 a month, and for the rest of this book, you will need it. $6.00 is a small price to pay for a program that can help you change your child's life. I recommend you continue to use RescueTime beyond this book, so you are more aware of your child's online time.

RescueTime Link: https://www.rescuetime.com/

Note: If you work with sensitive data, like classified data or HIPAA, then you cannot use RescueTime, as they store information about your activities. While they only store document names or website addresses, this could include sensitive information. If your child uses a device that you access that has sensitive information, do not install RescueTime.

What if I have an iPhone or an iPad?

Unfortunately, if you have an iPhone, iPad, or any device that uses iOS, RescueTime will not work. Something within iOS prohibits automatic record-ing needed for RescueTime to function. There are no alternatives that will automatically record the applications or websites you visit on iOS.

Fortunately, if you have iOS 12 or above, Apple has introduced Screen Time, which allows monitoring of your child's online activity. To enable it, click on Settings, then Screen Time. You can see how much time you have spent on your phone, as well as how much time for specific apps. You can see this information for today or the past seven days. You can see how you compare over time to see if your child's usage has decreased.

You can also sync this information across other Apple devices, allowing you to get an overall picture of your child's online usage. If your child has more than one Apple device they use, check this option. Screen Time even logs how many times your child has unlocked their device and how many notifications they have received. Apple's Screen Time is a useful and efficient method of tracking time across electronic devices. You can even set limits on how much time your child uses specific applications. Later in the book, when we discuss limiting your child's time online, you may want to do this to limit the time spent in specific applications.

Today's Activity

Determine if you can use RescueTime, and if so, install it on all supported devices. You will not be able to install these applications on all devices your child uses, such as game consoles and iPads. However, the more devices you can monitor, the better picture you will get about your child's online activities.

If you cannot install RescueTime, you need to log how much time your child spends on each application or game. It will be impossible to get a 100% accurate picture, as you cannot be with your child at all times. The goal is to get a general picture of how much time they spend online and what they are doing. If you cannot use RescueTime, I have created a log on my website you can use. The link is below:

Logbook Link: https://nathandriskell.com/child-addicted-electronics/online-hours-logbook-child-addicted-electronics.xlsx

Even if you have RescueTime, it will not help you record your time for gaming systems, Windows Phones, or other devices. You will need to add this information to RescueTime manually.

These next two days will likely be challenging and tedious. Cataloging your child's time will be frustrating for you and your child. They will likely become upset over this and view this as an invasion of privacy. However, you are their parent, their guardian, and you need to know what they are doing online. Talk to them first about the reasons behind this monitoring and how you will not remove all access to their games or applications. You will be limiting how much time they spend in these activities later, and this cataloging will determine what apps or games will be limited.

Quick To-Do List

1. Install RescueTime on all supported devices, if possible.
2. Monitor your child's online activity, including non-supported devices, as accurately as possible.

Tomorrow's Focus

At the end of the next two days, you will gain insight into your child's digital life. While two days is not a large sample, it is a snapshot of time that can give you an idea of how much time your child spends online. After these two days, you will analyze the data to determine what applications your child uses the most. Later in this book, you will learn **why** they engage in these activities to see what fuels their addiction.

DAY 7: DIGITAL FOOTPRINT, PART 3 – ANALYSIS

Now that you have spent the past two days cataloging your child's digital life, what did you find? Did they spend as much time online as you thought? Were their activities what you expected? You probably underestimated their online presence, and now you should have a better understanding of how much time your child's addiction is costing them.

While some time online is ok, your child needs a balance of activities. Spending too much time online will limit relationships, decrease communication skills, and make them more dependent on technology.

Today's Activity

For today's activity, you are going to make a list of the most time-consuming activities your child has conducted within the past two days. For this list, exclude any school, work, or meaningful activities. Include the top five activities that are time wasters, such as games, social media, texting, etc. For each item, put an average of how much time they spend on it daily by adding up the time spent for both days and dividing by 2.

Once this list is complete, you will know what activities you will need to limit your child. If they spend eight hours a day on social media, then this will be an area to reduce. If they spend 10 hours a day in an online game, this needs to change. There is a good chance the top activities on their list will not surprise you. What may be surprising is how much time they spend on them.

If you can use RescueTime, continue tracking their online usage while working through this book. Seeing how much time they spend online can tell you if the changes you have made are working. You need to keep RescueTime installed and running on all supported devices and each day log online activities that are not automatically cataloged, such as gaming consoles. If you cannot use RescueTime, continue to record your activity in the log you completed yesterday.

Quick To-Do List

1. Make a list of the five applications or websites that accounted for the most time spent the past two days. Add up the times for both days and divide by 2 to gain an average. Include the average with your list.
2. Continue to log your child's online activities daily by using your logbook or RescueTime.

Tomorrow's Focus

You now know how much time your child spends online and what applications and websites are the most problematic. With this knowledge, you will be able to make a plan to replace these applications with other more healthy alternatives. However, before we can make these changes, we need to get your family interacting again. To that end, tomorrow, you are going to plan a family outing, something you may not have done in some time. In planning this outing, you will take steps to get your family back together and having fun as a family. Continue monitoring your child's online activities, and be sure to take care of yourself in this process.

DAY 8: FAMILY DAY

Today you are going to take a break and focus on something fun. You will be meeting with your family to discuss something you can all do together. You will be scheduling something most likely on the weekend unless you can get your family together during the week. Expect your family to find this strange, and for some of them to object, as they may not be accustomed to spending time together.

No Electronics, Please

For the activity, try not to involve electronics or activities that are passive by nature. Examples include going to the movies, watching television, or other activities that do not require participation. The goal is to do things together as a family requiring communication. During the activity, keep access to electronics at a minimum, for parents as well as children.

Suggestions

Below are suggestions as to the activities you can do as a family. This list is by no means exhaustive. Show this list to your family, and have them choose which activity works best. If they want to do something not on this list, feel free.

- Go to the park.
- Drive someplace new.

- Go to a museum.
- Go to a sporting event.
- Go to the theater.
- Walk around the mall or some other large public place.
- Go to an amusement park.
- Go someplace different to eat.

Whatever you choose, make sure you can talk with your family during the activity or after. You want to get their opinions on the activity, as well as any thoughts or comments. Discussing the event on the way home is a good idea.

Do Not Expect Perfection

If you expect this day to go flawlessly, you are in for a rude awaking. Your children will not be used to this activity and will likely see it as a waste of time. Expect eye-rolling, sarcasm, or outright hostility. During the activity, expect minimal interaction, as they may shut you out as a form of protest.

Your child needs time to get used to other activities. For each Family Day, expect resistance. Over time, resistance will decrease as they find more activities they like. Be patient and give them time, and try not to become upset or angry if they are unpleasant during the activity.

Today's Activity

Tonight, schedule 10 minutes with your family to discuss an activity you can do together within the next few weeks. Make sure to let each family member give their opinions as to what they would like to do. Narrow it down to two choices, then vote as a family. Family members who did not win will help choose the next activity to feel included in the process. You can use the list of ideas in this chapter, or create your own.

Once you have scheduled the Family Day, wait to complete it before continuing this book. In the meantime, continuing monitoring your child's online access using RescueTime or the logbook and work to take care of your health.

Quick To-Do List

1. Spend 10 minutes with your family discussing an activity you can do as a family. Ensure this activity does not involve electronics and make sure it is something the family can do together. Once scheduled, have the Family Day, then be ready to resume this book.

Tomorrow's Focus

Hopefully, you have had your meeting and have planned a day soon with your family. After the Family Day, you are going to take a detailed look at your child's addiction, to see exactly how their addiction has affected them, you, and your family. You will research the games, apps, or online activities, to gain more knowledge of them. By knowing more about their online activities, you will begin to see why they conduct them, so you can help them find alternatives.

DAY 9: THE ADDICTION

Now that you have had your first Family Day, how did it go? Was it what you expected? How much resistance did your children give? What did you learn from it? Likely, it was an interesting experience that can be refined into something more positive and fun over time.

Today, you are going to be specific in looking at your child's addiction. You will take the list of activities you made on Day 7 and will learn more about each game or application on the list. While doing so, you will begin to look at things from your child's perspective, so you can see **why** they play the games or use the applications they do.

Knowledge = Power

For some of the games or applications on your list, you may not know much about them. You may have heard of them in passing, but do not understand what they are or how they work. Today, you will learn more about each game or application on your child's list, so you can learn why they may be addicted.

Some of these games and apps may be strange and difficult to understand. You may not understand what Snapchat is, or why someone would play League of Legends. Regardless of the application or game, you need to learn more about them. To do so, go to Google and search for the game or application. Wikipedia also has listings for games or applications. Reading articles about them will teach you more about their history and use.

Wikipedia Link: https://www.wikipedia.org/

You may need to spend a few hours in this research. If it takes more than a day, so be it. You need to be familiar with your child's online activities, so you can be better equipped to talk about them. If you research these applications or games, you can have a meaningful conversation with your child on what they gain from them.

Self Study

Once you have learned more about these activities, you will next do something radical. You will pick two of the activities on your child's list and use them for a brief time yourself. For example, if your child likes YouTube, and you have never been on it, you will begin using YouTube by searching for interests you like, then watching videos on them. If your child is on Snapchat, you will create an account then use it briefly to understand the experience.

You may think this is radical or extreme, as you may fear you might become addicted as well. Opening lines of communication requires you to know more about your child's online activities. Personal experience in these applications gives you the knowledge to help bridge the gap between you and your child. You want to see these applications from your child's eyes, to learn why they use them. Using these applications will teach you more about your child and their relationship to electronics.

Ask your child about these applications or games, and ask for help in accessing them. They may be surprised you are taking such an interest, or they may resist, feeling you are intruding into their world. Explain to them you want to learn more about their life, their activities and want to see things from their perspective. Playing a game with them or doing something together online may help them understand you are not against electronics but want to learn more about them.

Today's Activity

Begin your day by researching the five apps or games on the list you made on Day 7. Going to Wikipedia or the developers of the apps is a good starting point. Reading about them will give you an idea as to what they are and why they are popular.

Once you have researched all five activities, pick two of them, hopefully, ones you have not used before. Make a simple account, as most apps or games are free to play. If something is not free, you can choose to buy it, or ask your child if you can have access to theirs. Some games require subscriptions that can range from $10-$20 a month.

You may have resistance to completing today's task. You may feel this is counterintuitive, as you are reading this book to get help in managing your child's addiction, not participate in it. Playing a game or using an application your child is addicted to may feel wrong. However, the point is to learn more about your child's addiction and what they gain from it. You cannot learn this unless you have used the game or application to understand their allure. Electronics addiction is not like drugs or alcohol, you cannot abstain, and one use does not make you an addict. As an adult, you can control your actions and can make sure you do not become addicted. If you have an addiction to online games or social media, you can skip this step as you have personal experience with this addiction and what short-term gains it offers.

In completing today's activity, you will feel discomfort. This is normal and required. As I warned at the beginning of this book, it will not be easy to bring change to your child and your family. You are doing this to make your family better, and by understanding more about your child's addiction, you will be able to see what they gain from it.

Quick To-Do List

1. Research all five of the activities on your child's list from Day Seven. Do a Google search or go to Wikipedia to learn more about each activity.
2. Pick two of these activities, ones you have not done yourself, and try them. Make free accounts or ask your child to access theirs. Using these activities yourself, you will begin to see why your child uses them and what they gain. If you have addiction issues to games or electronics, skip this step.

Tomorrow's Focus

You are going to feel drained after today's activity. If you need a day or two to complete it, do so. Once done, you will begin to look at what your child gains from the addiction. As you have done two of these activities yourself, you will have a greater understanding of their viewpoints. Tomorrow, you will begin to learn more about what your child gains from electronics by discovering their Needs. In learning more about these Needs, you will help find alternatives so your child can better balance life and electronics.

DAY 10 & 11: NEEDS

You are beginning to learn more about what your child gains from their online activities. By trying two of their most time-consuming activities, you have a glimpse into their digital world. Today, you will go a step further by learning about Needs and how they impact human behavior. By learning about your child's Needs, you will begin to answer why they are addicted.

Everything we do as humans, we do for a reason. While some actions can be random, overall, we make choices on what we do. Even if something harms us, there is a benefit, at least in the short term. For children and adults alike, everything we do, we gain something from it.

For example, take someone who is an alcoholic. Everyone knows drinking to excess is damaging and destructive. While there may be short-term benefits, long-term consequences can be devastating. If the alcoholic knows this, why does he drink? He knows he is damaging his life, his relationships with others, and will eventually lose everything. He drinks because he gains a short-term benefit. It may be too dull a pain he has experienced in the past. It may be to feel more social. Whatever the reason, he drinks because he gains a short-term benefit he does not know how to fulfill by other means.

Therefore, everything we do helps us in the short-term, even if it harms us in the long term. Remember this quote, as it is a reason why your child is addicted to electronics. Their online activities are providing them with a benefit, one that has become an addiction. The question is, what Needs do they gain from them?

What are Needs?

A Need is something we require as a person to feel complete. Everyone has Needs, which can include physical constructs such as food, shelter, safety, etc. Needs also include relationships, the search for meaning, relaxation, and affection. Needs are the basis of human existence. We exist to fulfill these Needs and will spend most of our lives in the pursuit of them.

While many of our Needs overlap, everyone's Needs are unique. If I were to make a list of Needs and compare it with yours, our lists would be different. We all have different value systems, each just as unique as our Needs. Addictions form to fulfill a Need, even if it is destructive.

When I spent six years addicted to an online game, my Needs for this game included self-esteem, control, power, and connection. In the game, I was one of the most powerful players. I spent much of my time becoming more powerful so that I could feel better about myself. The game supplied my Need for connection, as I had many friends, in contrast to my real life. The game provided my Needs for control and power, as I knew how to win, and felt stronger than most of my peers. Because I was influential and well known, my self-esteem improved. The game supplied my Needs, even though the game was not real. In my mind, the game was more important than real life, and I did not care how I met my Needs.

For me to quit the game, I had to understand what I gained from it. By knowing self-esteem was an issue, I started to change how I thought about myself. By gaining more confidence in myself, I was able to gain more control over my life. This control leads to power, as I felt in charge of my life. Once I quit the game, I focused on real-world alternatives to supply my Needs.

List of Needs

Below is a list of Needs grouped by a common theme. You will use this list to determine the possible Needs your child's addiction supplies. You can choose as many Needs as you feel relate to their addiction.

Connection
Acceptance
Affection
Appreciation
Belonging
Cooperation
Communication
Closeness
Community
Companionship
Consideration
Consistency
Empathy
Inclusion
Intimacy
Love
Mutuality
Nurturing
Respect
Self-Respect
Safety
Security
Stability
Support
To Know
To See
To Understand

Trust

Warmth

Physical

Air

Food

Exercise

Sleep

Sex

Safety

Shelter

Touch

Water

Honesty

Authenticity

Integrity

Presence

Play

Joy

Humor

Peace

Beauty

Communication

Ease

Equality

Harmony

Inspiration

Order

Autonomy

Choice
Freedom
Independence
Space
Spontaneity

Meaning
Awareness
Challenge
Clarity
Competence
Consciousness
Contribution
Creativity
Discovery
Efficacy
Effectiveness
Growth
Hope
Learning
Mourning
Participation
Purpose
Stimulation
Understanding

This list was created by the Center for Nonviolent Communication:
  © 2005 by Center for Nonviolent Communication
  Website: www.cnvc.org E-Mail: cnvc@cnvc.org
  Phone: +1.505-244-4041

This list is a sample; there are more Needs than these. If a Need is not on this list, list it regardless.

Today's Activity

For the next two days, you will observe your child while they are online while using the list of Needs above to determine what they gain from their online activities. At times you will talk to them about what they are doing and how they feel while completing these activities.

Your child will likely find this strange, as they may not be aware of what they feel beyond enjoyment. Go over the five applications or games you listed on Day 7, asking your child what Needs they gain from them. You can use an activity you do as an example, by listing the Needs you gain. Do not judge or blame your child for the Needs they choose; everyone has Needs. Hopefully, this conversation will open up a dialog for you and your child, so they can feel more comfortable in discussing their online activities.

Quick To-Do List

1. For the next two days, note the Needs for each activity on your child's list from Day 7, and begin to discuss these Needs with your child, so they are more comfortable discussing their online activities.

Tomorrow's Focus

After observing your child and talking to them about their Needs, you have a better understanding of why they are addicted. For your child to break this addiction, they need to understand what they gain from their addiction, so they can begin to find real-world alternatives. As a parent, your job is to assist them in this process by providing activities and encouragement. For many children, the Internet and electronics are coping skills to deal with life's stress and pressures. While the Internet can be a great short-term coping skill, long-term use forms addiction. To that end, your child needs to learn better coping skills. Tomorrow, you will learn more about healthy coping skills so you can teach them to your child.

DAY 12: HEALTHY COPING SKILLS

A s parents, we often forget how stressful life can be for our children. Children go to school for around eight hours a day, then have homework and other obligations. As different stages, their bodies change, causing confusion and chaos. On top of this, technology has affected how children develop. Children of this generation are dealing with conditions never before present. As most have been born into technology, their place in the world is different than all who came before.

Parents cannot personally understand this level of technology and the pressures it creates. Bullying, for example, is an age-old problem that has magnified tenfold due to technology and social media. Children can be bullied 24 hours a day, in school and at home, all on social media. Due to this, our children are under extreme stress, and pressure adults do not understand.

As a result, many of our children have dove into electronics and the Internet, forming a coping skill to deal with the pain and stress. For children to reduce their time online, they will need to learn new coping skills. This chapter will teach you, the parent, how to use these coping skills so that you can teach them to your child. We warned, some of these coping skills may seem strange, and all require practice to use correctly.

Grounding

The first coping skill you will learn is grounding. Grounding is one of the few coping skills you can practice anywhere. It is quick, convenient, and powerful. I have seen grounding work for people with ADHD, PTSD, Schizophrenia, Depression, and Addiction. Grounding is one of the most powerful coping skills you can learn.

What is grounding? Grounding involves using the five senses to focus on what is happening at the moment. We often get caught up in one feeling at a time, while ignoring what our bodies tell us. If we crave stimulation, say from an online game, we may ignore how tired we are, or our body temperature, or physical pain. Grounding helps tune into what our bodies are telling us, as well as a breaking point for our focus. For example, if I have a craving to play an online game, then use a grounding technique, I have distracted myself from the craving, giving my mind time to find an alternative.

To begin grounding, you will use all five senses to describe the world around you. The technique has a set order and method you need to memorize. It is quite simple and should be easy to remember after the first few times. For example, you will describe five objects you see. For each object, describe its characteristics. The more detail you provide, the better. Below is an example:

Object: A box fan

"I see a fan. It has a square shape, but the corners are round. It is white with its blades spinning quickly. There is a grill over the fan with slats for the air to come out. On top of the fan is a gray knob you turn to adjust the fan's speed. The fan has a white handle on top."

I could have said, "I see a white fan," but this is not enough detail. The more effort you put into the description, the better grounding will work.

You will begin with five things you see, followed by four things you feel. Next, you will describe three things you hear, followed by two things you smell. You will end with one thing you taste. The order and amount of objects do not change.

Sight

To begin, focus on objects you see in your environment. The objects them-selves do not matter, as long as they are real, physical objects. Good examples are paintings, furniture, plants, dishes, papers, and electronics. Describe them in detail to yourself. You do not need to speak out loud; you can think of these descriptions. The power of grounding is its portability. No one needs to know you are doing it. Below is another example of how I would describe an object:

Object: A small digital picture frame

"I see a digital picture frame. The frame portion is black, and overall it is a rectangle. It is maybe 7 inches across. The picture changes every 10 seconds, and the screen is backlit. A black cord extends from the picture frame to the wall. Each picture is different, mostly from nature or museums I have visited in the past".

The description above gives a good mental picture of the picture frame. The more time you focus on your descriptions, the better you will be at distracting from a craving or a moment of anxiety. Describe five different objects in your environment in a similar manner.

Feel

You will now describe how you feel in four different areas. These include physical sensations, such as hunger, pain, temperature, and feelings, such as anxiety, sadness, or happiness. It is best to try to get a mix of feelings, so you know how your body feels physically and emotionally. Below is an example of an internal feeling:

Internal feeling: Anxiety

"I feel somewhat anxious right now. I feel this because I am about to speak in front of a group, and I am afraid of how it will go. This anxiety feels like butterflies in my stomach, and my foot is tapping as a way to distract myself from it".

In the example above, anxiety was the feeling of speaking in front of a group. The cause, speaking in front of a group, lead to the feeling of anxiety. A physical sensation of butterflies in the stomach preceded the feeling. The foot-tapping was interesting, as it could be a small coping skill designed to lessen the anxiety.

Below is an example of a physical feeling:

Physical feeling: Hot

"I feel hot right now due to the heat in my office. It is around 100 degrees outside, and my air conditioner is not up to the task. I feel sweet on my back and stomach, and I feel wet all over. It is an annoying feeling I do not like".

In this example, the physical feeling, hot was caused by the outside temperature and an underpowered air conditioner. Physical sensations such as feeling sweet on the stomach and wetness describe more feelings. This example also included a response to this physical sensation, the feeling of annoyance. By knowing this feeling, actions can be taken to lessen the annoyance, such as getting a glass of water. Let your example follow this format. Now, describe four things you feel, with a mix of internal and external feelings.

Hear

Next, turn to the sounds you hear in the environment. This one may prove more difficult as we often discount background noise. You may need to sit quietly for a few moments and focus on the sounds around you. Below is an example:

"I hear the noisemaker outside my office door. It is a consistent sound, and it is slightly loud. The sound is of static used to drawn-out sounds from within my office. It is easy to ignore".

In this example, the source of the noise is mentioned and how loud it was. The last portion, easy to ignore, describes how important the sound is. Most of the sounds you hear will be background sounds you will easily dismiss. However, knowing they are there allows you to be more aware of your surroundings and distract you from yourself. Go ahead and focus on three sounds you hear near you, describing as I have above.

Smell

The further down the list we go, the more focus it takes to describe our senses. As most of our senses produce only background information, it takes more mental energy to focus. It may prove difficult to distinguish two different smells, as we often blend them in our minds. Below is an example of two different smells:

Smells: Pine & Ketchup

"I smell a sort of cleaning agent, something with pine. It is a faint smell that I did not notice unless I focus. There is another smell in the room; I think it is of ketchup. It is a tangy smell but extremely faint as if it was present hours ago. The pine smell is easier to distinguish, but the ketchup smell is present if I focus. I do not like the combination of the smells together, but I can ignore it as both smells are slight".

Notice how I describe how the smells work together, as well as how strong they are. I noted how I felt about the smells, which is useful as part of this exercise is to observe your feelings. I described the possible sources for the smells, even though I was not entirely sure. Go ahead and describe two smells you smell right now.

Taste

The last sense, taste, may be easy or difficult, depending on how long it has been since you had something to eat or drink. Taste and smell are linked, and something you described for smell may also be present in taste. If this is the case, focus on a different taste, as we often can taste more than one thing at a time. Below is an example:

Taste example: Mint

"I taste a mint I had around 2 hours ago before I left for my office. It is a slight flavor that has decreased over time. It is a pleasant flavor that takes the place of the pasta I had for lunch. It is fading and will not last much longer".

I noted the taste, the possible source of the taste, and what I thought about it. I also included how long I believe the taste will last. Go ahead and try for yourself.

Once you have completed all five senses, ask yourself how you feel and what you want to focus on next. The point of the grounding exercise is to distract yourself from the negative feeling or urge you are experiencing. Focus on something you need to do, then take steps to complete it. If you still feel this urge, repeat the grounding exercise until you feel more in control. Grounding takes time to practice and get right. You will not be an expert in a week.

Equal Breathing (Deep Breathing Exercise)

Everyone knows how to breathe, but did you know we often do it wrong? We often breathe in one breath for a second or two, then exhale and repeat. We often do not get enough oxygen in our bodies, stressing our brains. Learning how to control your breathing will help reduce stress and improve your overall functioning.

While there are numerous deep breathing exercises, you will learn the easiest and most accessible. Equal breathing is a simple exercise you can use anywhere, just like grounding. You can do it in the car, at your desk at work, or in public. To perform an equal breathing exercise, do the following:

1. Notice your natural breath, and calmly take note of how long each breath takes.
2. Take one breath and count to four, holding the breath. Note how you feel when you reach four.
3. Exhale slowly, counting to four. Note how you feel when your breath is empty.
4. Repeat steps 2-3 for 5-10 minutes, making sure your inhales and exhales are around the same length.

Over time you can increase the count if you wish. The more you practice, the longer you will be able to hold your breath without distraction. At first, it won't be easy to match your breaths without complete focus, but it will become more natural over time. After years of practice, some people can breathe this way automatically.

Like grounding, practice equal breathing often. Use it when stressed or before something unpleasant. Equal breathing also works well before bed, and if you cannot sleep. Combining equal breathing and meditation is recommended. Speaking of meditation...

Meditation

Meditation has gotten a bad rap as something with mats and silly poses. Meditation, in the terms I will describe, is an activity where you clear your mind of thoughts and expectations. I used to think meditation was pointless until I experienced it firsthand.

Meditation is the act of clearing your mind in a controlled manner. You can use guided meditation, where a narrator is giving you instructions or affirmations. You can use musical meditation, where you listen to soothing sounds to help clear your mind. The key is repeating this behavior daily for at least two months until it forms into a habit.

In the beginning, it won't be easy to clear your mind, as you have had little practice doing so. We are often undisciplined with our thoughts and allow ourselves to get swept up in them. Meditation is learning to control your thoughts. The more practice, the easier it becomes to block out intrusive thoughts.

Below is a list of free online resources that can help you meditate. Some, like Pandora, have meditation channels which sometimes have advertisements. Try the different channels and determine what works for you:

- Pandora: Online music service. Search for Meditation and try the different channels: http://www.pandora.com/
- Spotify: Online music service. Search for Meditation or Guided Meditation channels. https://www.spotify.com/
- YouTube: Video playing service. Search for Guided Meditation or Meditation music. https://www.youtube.com/

Today's Activity

Today, you are going to begin to develop a meditation routine and practice grounding and equal breathing. While working in this book, pick a time of the day you can meditate for 15 minutes. During your meditation period, you will be alone, with no distractions. You can choose to use calming music, use a guided meditation exercise, or use your choice of music.

As you meditate, focus on the music or instructions you hear. Do not focus on your problems, your tasks, or your day. If you feel sleepy, resist this urge and do an equal breathing exercise. Keep yourself focused on the music you hear, and let yourself drift from thoughts about yourself. Equal breathing while meditating will help keep you focused and enhance the experience.

Each day you will also practice the grounding and equal breathing exercises you learned above. Grounding and equal breathing are perfect for moments where you feel anxious or distracted. Try to practice both at least ten times a day, until they become easy. You will use grounding and equal breathing to help calm down during stressful situations.

As you learn these coping skills, you are going to teach them to your child. Expect resistance, as they will likely think them stupid or dumb. Meditation, for example, can be an activity the family does together for 15 minutes in the evening until everyone has learned it. Do not expect perfection; your child is not used to these coping skills. All three coping skills above have been tested and used for years and have done wonders to reduce stress and anxiety. The more coping skills your child learns, the less they will depend on electronics to manage stress.

Quick To-Do List

1. Begin to meditate daily by choosing a time when you will not be distracted, then spend 15 minutes listening to music or guided meditation. Focus on the music, not yourself or your responsibilities.
2. Practice grounding and equal breathing at least ten times a day, during times you need to calm down or gain focus.
3. Begin to teach your child these coping skills, knowing it will take time, and there will be resistance. It may take months, but in the end, it will be worth it.

Tomorrow's Focus

You have reached the end of Part 1 of this book. Hopefully, you have learned more about your child's addiction and have begun to spend more time with your family. The next section will focus on the actions you will take to combat your child's addiction to electronics. Expect resistance and difficulty, as you will be making radical changes for all members of your family. While it will be difficult, over time, your children will become used to these changes. Continue to monitor your child's online activities and practice the coping skills learned in this chapter, as you will need them in the days ahead.

PART 2: ACTION

DAY 13: THE CONTRACT – PART 1

T oday is a big day. You are going to begin creating a framework for your child's daily life. The framework will include limiting electronic access, sleep and wake schedules, proper use of electronics, and developing new hobbies. From now on, you will begin to implement this framework day by day until complete.

You will have help in this process, for your child is going to assist you. To that end, you will create a contract with your child that highlights rules relating to online access. At first, your child will resist you in placing limits on their online time. However, they will compromise, as limited online access is preferable to none.

Another Meeting

Today, you will conduct another family meeting. Ensure all members are present, as this contract is not just for your child but also for everyone in the household. All parents need to be present, if possible, as limits will be placed on parents' online access. Your children will have more motivation to abide by the contract rules if it also affects parents. If your child is handed a list of rules with no input, they will ignore them as they will feel they had no say. Your child needs to feel invested in this process, so they will feel it is fair.

Rules of Access

While creating this contract, focus on specifics in regards to access. For example, one rule could be that there will be no electronics at the dinner table. Be specific, such as there will be no electronics for all meals or while completing homework at the dinner table. You can expand this rule to include meals in restaurants or with extended family.

Think of when you will allow access to electronics, and when you will not. The contract has to include times when online time is ok. Remember, your children's goal is to learn how to balance electronics with life and not remove all access. Having limited access to games or social media is allowed. I suggest allowing two hours of electronic access a day for weekdays, with four hours for weekends or holidays. This should be enough time for videos, games, and social media.

Remember, the contract has to include limits on parents' online time as well. If you have set a limit of no electronics in your children's rooms past a certain time, you need to do the same for parents. If your children do not see rules limiting your behavior, they will not follow theirs.

Resistance

You may feel angry at the suggestion of limiting your online time. You may be thinking, "I am not the one with the problem, so why should I have to change my behavior?". The simple answer is: you are the model of appropriate behavior. As a parent, it is your job to show your children how to balance life with electronics. On Day 2, I asked what your addictions were, as you need to make changes in your life. You may also be addicted to electronics, or at times abuse them. By setting healthy limitations on your time, your life will improve, and your children will notice.

This process will not be easy for you or your child. Before you create the contract, you need to sit down and think about your online use and what changes you will need to make. In the meeting, be honest with your usage, and set limits on your access. By limiting your access, your child will feel better, as they will not think everything is about them.

Sample Contract

Below is a sample contract to give you an idea of the areas to cover. Do not use this example for your own, as you need to design it with input from your family. Some of the items below are areas we will tackle as we work through this book.

Electronics Usage Contract

Children:

Rule 1: Cell Phone, Tablets, and other electronics will not be in bedrooms past 9:00 PM on school nights, and 11:00 PM on weekends. Electronics will be returned to parents at this time and will be given back the following morning.

Rule 2: Electronics will be given back in the morning, once hygiene tasks are complete, and the child is ready for school or weekend activities.

Rule 3: No electronics will be present at the dinner table, unless permitted by the parents, for school or other productive purposes.

Rule 4: No electronics will be out in the open in the car or any vehicle unless used for GPS. Electronics will be put up in pockets or given to parents.

Rule 5: No electronics will be out in the open during family outings. Electronics will be in pockets or given to parents.

Rule 6: Electronics will not be used during family time; this includes: watching

TV, family discussions, and other activities in the home or outside of the home.

Rule 7: On school nights, electronics are limited to two hours per day. On weekends or holidays, electronics are limited to four hours a day. This time can be increased or decreased due to grades and performance at home.

Rule 8: Electronics are free to be used for an hour after children get home from school, and for an hour once homework is complete.

Parents:

Rule 1: Parents will stop using electronics past 10:00 PM on weekdays and midnight on weekends unless engaged in work-related activity or a family-related activity.

Rule 2: Parents will not use electronics until they have completed hygiene-related tasks and are ready for the workday or weekend activities.

Rule 3: No electronics will be present at the dinner table unless it is for work-related purposes.

Rule 4: No electronics will be out in the car unless using GPS.

Rule 5: Parents will not use electronics on family outings unless needed for the outing.

Rule 6: Electronics will not be used during family time unless on call for work, or the electronics are needed for family time.

As you can see, many of the parent rules are similar to the children's rules. Creating the contract this way shows your children the contract is not all about them. Your contract will not look exactly like the one above, but be sure you have a section for children and parents, so all see it as fair.

Today's Activity

Go ahead and schedule the meeting for the creation of the contract. Do not proceed with this book until you have had the meeting, as the contract is vital to continue. Give about an hour to have this meeting, and be prepared to write down a rough draft of this contract. Once you have a rough draft, type it out, and make changes as needed. Once your family agrees to the contract, print it out, and have each member sign it. Keep it in a public place, such as on the refrigerator. You can edit the contract as needed; however, make sure all members know the changes and have some input. Towards the end of the book, you will have another meeting, where your family can discuss changes to the contract.

Quick To-Do List

1. Schedule a meeting with your family and create a contract for electronics usage. Use the sample in this chapter as a beginning point. Ensure each member of your family has input in the contract and make sure a section contains parents' rules.

Tomorrow's Focus

With the contract complete, you have begun to limit access to electronics. The next few weeks will be difficult as your children will test the limits of this contract. Make sure there are consequences for breaking the rules of the contract and do not budge from them. Setting these boundaries is critical in changing your child's behavior.

During the next three days, you will use the list of electronics from Day 4 and begin to lock down each device your child uses. This includes PC's, phones, and tablets. You will go through each device, learn about all the applications they use, and give yourself access to these devices. For your child's safety, you will install monitoring software, so you are aware of their activities on these devices. By limiting their access and knowing what they do online, you will help keep your children safe.

DAY 14 - 16: LOCK DOWN ELECTRONICS

Today, you are going to take control of the electronics your children use. You will do this for all children, not just the one addicted to electronics. As you do for one child, you must do it for all. Your other children will likely become angry and resist; however, over time, their lives will be more balanced as well.

Take the list of all electronics your child uses you made on Day 4, and add any devices you forgot. Make a similar list for each child and prepare to gather these devices so you can gain access to them.

Personal Computers

For each personal computer in your home your children use, you will need to collect their user account information. Account information includes usernames, e-mail addresses, and passwords. You will make a list of this information to use later if you need to access their accounts.

To ensure access to their accounts, you need to remove your child's ability to change their password. If your child wants to change their password, you will have to do it for them. For Windows 7, 8, 8.1, and 10 computers, do the following:

1. Log in to the computer as an Administrator.
2. For Windows 7, press the Windows Key, then type "Computer Manage-ment" and click it when it appears. On Windows 8+, press the Windows Key than X, and choose "Computer Management" from the menu.
3. On the left side of the window, click "Local Users and Groups."
4. Double Click "Users" on the right.
5. Right Click on your child's username and select "Properties."
6. Check the following box: "User cannot change password."
7. Hit the "OK" button, then close all windows and reboot the computer.

Your child can no longer change their password unless you change it for them. If you have an older PC, you can search on Google to help you locate the password. There are too many possibilities to include in this book.

If you have a MAC, this will be difficult, as there is no easy way to lock down passwords. Some versions of OS X allow this; others do not. If you own a MAC, find your OS X version, then do a Google search to see if you can prevent users from changing the password. You may need a 3rd party application to do this.

I also suggest limiting your child's account so it is not an Administrator, so they cannot change their settings, giving them the ability to change their passwords. For Windows 10, 8, 8.1, and 7 computers do the following:

1. Log in to the computer as an Administrator.
2. On Windows 7, press the Windows Key and then choose "Control Panel" from the menu. On Windows 8+, press the Windows Key than X, to bring up a menu, and then select "Control Panel" from the menu.
3. You will most likely be in Category view. If so, you need to switch to Large Icons. To do so, look for "View by:" and next to this, choose "Large Icons." If you are already in "Large Icons" or "Small Icons" view, ignore this step.
4. Next, Click on "User Accounts."
5. Now, Click on "Manage another account."

6. Click on your child's account.
7. Click on "Change the account type."
8. Choose "Standard" as you do not want your child to be an Administrator.
9. Click on the "Change Account Type" Button, then close all windows and reboot the computer.

Do this for all of your children, so they are no longer Administrators. They will be able to install most software, but will not be allowed to edit other users or make system-wide changes. As a parent, your account needs to be the Administrator, so you have full control over their accounts.

Phones and Tablets

For your children's phones and tablets, make a list of their user accounts. If it is an Android device, you will record their Gmail account and password. If it is an Apple device, write down their Apple ID and password. By having these ID's, you will be able to log into their devices so you can see the apps they use, and will be able to control them.

If your child has an iPhone, iPad, or iPod touch, you can set parental controls and limit or block specific apps and features. To enable parental controls, do the following:

1. On their device, Tap "Settings," then "General," then "Restrictions."
2. Tap "Restrictions," then tap "Enable Restrictions."
3. You will now create a restrictions passcode. With a restrictions passcode, your child will be unable to change settings unless you put in your passcode. Create a passcode you will remember, as if you forget, you will need to erase the device and start over.
4. You will now be able to restrict applications and settings. Make sure you disable Installing Apps, Deleting Apps, and In-App Purchases. With these services disabled, your child will not be able to install applications, delete them, or purchase items within applications without inputting

the passcode you created earlier.

5. Go through the other options each and determine if you want your child to have access. If you do not know what an application or setting does, do a Google search to learn more about it.

With these restrictions in place, your child will no longer be able to use the applications or settings you do not want. You may need to spend some time researching each application.

Prevent Installation of Applications

Later in this book, you will remove or disable your child's five most-used applications from their mobile devices. Once you do, you will need a way to prevent your child from reinstalling these applications. If you own an iOS device, follow the previous section's instructions to disable the installation of applications. If you own an Android device, this becomes a difficult task, as there is no setting to remove the installation of applications for all Android devices. To do so, you will need parental control software.

Parental Control Software

For cell phones and tablets, it's hard to monitor and lock down these devices with default settings within the software. While you can lock some things down, an application is needed to gain full control over the device. For Android devices, this is particularly the case, as there are many different versions.

To that end, finding parental control software that locks down content, disables the installation of applications, and tracks usage history is ideal. There are many different applications to try, some free, but most require yearly subscriptions. Below is a list of the most common applications:

- **Norton Family Premier Link**: https://us.norton.com/norton-family-premier

63

- **Phone Sheriff Link**: http://www.phonesheriff.com/
- **ESET Parental Control For Android Link**: https://play.google.com/store/apps/details?id=com.eset.parental&hl=en
- **Net Nanny Link**: https://www.netnanny.com/
- **Qustodio Link**: https://www.qustodio.com/en/

A review from Tom's Guide, a website specializing in technology reviews, rated Norton Family Premier as the best Android application, with Net Nanny being the best overall. You can find this review at the link below. I suggest researching applications to determine which one works for you. I have had experience with Norton Family Premier from Clients who said they would recommend it.

Best Parental Control Apps Review: http://www.tomsguide.com/us/best-parental-control-apps,review-2258.html

If you own an Android device, I suggest Norton Family Premier. Below are the features for Android:

- Track search activities within the Norton Browser, so you know what your child searches.
- Track what websites your child visits and create rules for what can be accessed.
- Parents get alerts if their child breaks a rule.
- Track the location of your child's phone via GPS.
- See what applications are installed and take control over them.
- Choose who your children can text and monitor their text messages.
- Limit the amount of time your child can use his or her device.
- 30-day activity report, showing your child's usage.
- Instant Locking, where you can enable or lock down the device at any time.

With Norton Family Premier installed, you will have ultimate control over your child's phone. You can install an application on your phone or use a web browser to control your child's phone. You will be able to monitor access and see alerts from anywhere.

The drawback for Norton Family Premier, or any other parental control application, is the configuration. It will take time to set up and learn the software. Before you install parental control software, go to the manufacturer's website, and read the instructions. If you do not set it up correctly, your child may be able to gain access or disable it. Expect to spend an evening installing and configuring the software.

For iOS, Norton Family Premier is also available and includes many of the same features as the Android version, with notable exceptions. You cannot limit text messages, as Apple does not permit applications to do this. Also, their location tracking is limited and sometimes gives incorrect results. Lastly, you cannot set time restrictions for applications, meaning there is no way to limit how much time your child can use a particular application. For iOS, Net Nanny or Qustodio may be a better fit.

Norton Family Premier is at this writing $49.99 for a year's subscription. They offer a 30-day trial. I suggest using the 30-day free trial to evaluate it for yourself. If you find it works for you, pay for the full version. If not, try the other alternatives on this list and see what works best.

Before you continue this book, I highly recommend installing parental control software on all your child's mobile devices. You need a method to take control and limit access. Before installing this application, talk with your child about the reasons for it and why you feel the application is needed. Do not install this application behind their back, or you will damage their trust in you. The goal is not to spy on your child but to be aware of their activities and help keep them safe. Install the application of your choice, monitor it weekly to make sure it is working, as no one application will catch everything.

Gaming Consoles

Locking down your child's gaming consoles will take some work as well. You may have done this when you first got the console. If you have not, follow the instructions below for each gaming console to enable parental controls:

XBOX One

First, you need to create an account for yourself if you do not already have one. To create an account on the Xbox One, you will need a Microsoft Account. If you have a Windows PC, you may already have a Microsoft Account. If you do not have a Microsoft Account, follow the link below to sign up for one. Once you have created a Microsoft Account, you can create your user account on the Xbox One. To do so, follow the link below. Make sure you and your child both have accounts, as you will limit access to their account.

Microsoft Account Signup Link: https://account.microsoft.com/account/Account?lang=en-US&refd=account.live.com&refp=landing&destrt=home-index

Xbox One User Creation Guide: https://support.xbox.com/en-US/xbox-one/security/add-family-member-on-xbox-one

Once you and your child's accounts are created, you can begin locking down your child's account. To do so, follow the instructions below:

1. Log into your parent account on the XBOX One.
2. Go to Xbox One Settings Page.
3. Select the Gamertag for your child's account.
4. Go through each of the following options: Privacy and Online Safety on Xbox one. If you also have an Xbox 360, you can edit these settings as well. For the above options, go through them and determine the access you want for your child. Conduct a Google search if you do not understand

some of the options.

5. Click Save once done, then log out and have your child log in for the settings to take effect.

You will now have your child's account locked down. If you wish to revise settings, log back into your account, and make any changes needed. Ensure that you have password-protected your account, and your child does not know the password, so they cannot change these settings. For each child who uses the Xbox One, follow these instructions.

PlayStation 4

Like the Xbox One, you can enable parental controls to limit the content your child can access on the PlayStation 4. The first step is to create a parent account for yourself if you do not already have one. To do so, follow the instructions below:

1. Select "New User," then "Create a User."
2. Select "Next." You will be asked if you are new to the PlayStation Network. If you already have a PlayStation Network ID, you can use this ID. If not, choose "Create an Account" then "Sign Up Now."
3. Enter your details and preferences, then select "Next."
4. Now, create an Online ID, then enter your first and last name. Be careful, once created, you cannot change your Online ID.
5. You can now choose your Sharing, Friends, and Messages settings. You can skip these for now if you wish.
6. Read and accept the PlayStation Network Terms of Service.
7. Check your e-mail for a verification e-mail, then click it.
8. Your account has been created. Sign in with this account so that you can begin sub-accounts for your children.

Now that your account has been set up and verified, you can create sub-accounts for each of your children so that you can control their access to the PlayStation Network. For some children, you may not want online access. To create sub-accounts, follow the instructions below:

1. On the PS4 Home Screen, go to "Settings," then "Parental Controls," and enter your PlayStation Network account password.
2. Select "Sub Account Management," then "Add Child," then "Next."
3. You should see a list of users. Select your child's account, or choose "Create User" if their account has not been created yet.
4. Enter your child's name and date of birth, if they are empty.
5. Now, enter an e-mail address.
6. You can choose to allow PlayStation Network access or to have it disabled.
7. If you have allowed access to the PlayStation Network, you can create your child's Online ID and enter their e-mail address, if they have not already done so.
8. Your child's account should be ready for use.

Once you have limited access, you can begin setting parental controls for all users on the PlayStation 4. The Playstation 4 uses age ranges to determine access. Depending on your child's age, they will only be able to access content suited for it. Below is a table of the age ranges and their corresponding access level:

Players Age

Age: Under 3 Access Level: 1
Age: 3-6 Access Level: 2
Age: 7-11 Access Level: 3
Age: 12-15 Access Level: 4
Age: 16-17 Access Level: 5
Age: 18+ Access Level: 6

For example, if your child is 12, selecting level 5 would allow them to see content for ages 12 and below. As your child ages, you can allow different levels of content. **Note**, Parental controls cannot be set per user, meaning these are system-wide settings. Set parental controls based on the youngest child in your home. You can adjust these settings later for access for older children.

To restrict access to games, applications, and downloaded films, do the following:

1. From the Playstation 4's home screen, press up on the d-pad to go to the Function area.
2. Go to "Settings," then "Parental Controls," then "Restrict Use of PS4 Features", then "Application," and choose the level you would like to set based on the table above.
3. When you set parental controls for the first time, you will create a passcode consisting of four numbers. Make sure your child does not know this passcode so that you can make these changes yourself.

You can set limits on Blu-Ray Moves, DVD Movies, and the Internet Browser as well, by doing the steps above, under "Restrict Use of PS4 Features" and choosing "Blu-Ray," "DVD Movies," or "Internet Browser."

It is a good idea to also restrict your child from logging into your user account, so they cannot change these settings. Ensure your user account is password protected with a password they do not know, so they cannot log in as you and make changes.

Nintendo Wii U

Configuring the Wii U's parental controls is not difficult. To begin, ensure that you have created a user account for yourself, as you will use this account to lock down your children's accounts. To create your user account, follow the instructions below:

1. First, log into your child's account.
2. Access "User Settings" on an existing Mii (Username), then select "Create / Link Nintendo Network ID."
3. Select "Add New User" from the Wii U User Select Screen.
4. Select "Next" to continue through the screens.
5. If you already have a Nintendo ID, you can use this ID for your User Account. You may have one if you have used a Nintendo Wii or 3DS. If not, select "No" when asked if you already have a Nintendo Network ID.
6. Select "Next."
7. You will now create a "Mii," which is an avatar that will represent you. It does not matter how it looks; you can change things later.
8. Now, choose your language.
9. Read the Nintendo Network Agreement, then select "I Accept" to continue.
10. Select "OK" to continue.
11. Enter your Birthdate, then select "Next."
12. Select your Gender, your State, and Time Zone. Tap "OK" to continue.
13. If you do not yet have a Nintendo Network ID, you will create it now. You cannot change this later, so be careful in naming your ID. Enter a Nintendo Network ID, then select "OK" twice to continue.
14. You will now create a password for your Nintendo Network ID. Once you create the password, you will input it twice. Once done, select "OK" twice to continue.
15. Verify if you want to access Nintendo Network Services from other devices.
16. Next, enter your e-mail address, then select "OK."
17. Enter your e-mail address again to verify, then select "OK."
18. Verify if you would like to receive communication from Nintendo and its partners.
19. Review all information and verify it is correct. Select "OK" twice to confirm.
20. A confirmation e-mail will be sent to your e-mail address. Check your e-mail and follow the instructions to verify your account.

21. Your account is now complete, which you can also link to a Nintendo DS if your child has one.

Once you have created your account, follow the instructions below to enable parental controls:

1. Log into your account.
2. Open the Parental Controls channel on the Wii U Menu. The first time you open the channel, it will ask you to create a four-digit pin. Create a passcode your children do not know. Make sure an e-mail address has been set up on your account, as you can use your e-mail address to reset your pin if you forget it in the future.
3. Next, you will create a secret question you can answer if you forget your pin. Choose a question from the list, then remember the answer if someday you forget your pin.
4. Once done, you will be able to make any changes or begin setting up parental controls for specific applications. To go Parental Control Settings to start.
5. Now, select your child's account, then start looking through the applications to determine which ones you want to limit. Conduct a Google search if you need help learning about a game or application.

Complete this for all your children who use the Wii U, so you will have more control over the types of games and applications they use. You may want to disable the Internet Browser on all game consoles if you feel your children are accessing websites you would prefer them not to.

Nintendo Switch

For the Switch, Nintendo has made it easy to access and configure parental controls. Nintendo has created a Parental Controls mobile application to download on your Android or iOS device to configure and monitor the Nintendo Switch.

The Parental Controls Mobile Application has the following capabilities:

- Limit the amount of time each day the Switch is on.
- Limit access to the Switch for specific times.
- The Switch can suspend the console when it goes past the time limits set.
- Limit access to features and games based on age.
- Limit the ability to post screenshots of games to social media.
- Limit sharing of in-game text or images.

To download the application, use your iOS or Android device. Links are provided below:

Android Google Play: https://play.google.com/store/apps/details?id=com.nintendo.znma&gl=us&hl=en

iOS App Store: https://itunes.apple.com/us/app/id1190074407

Download and install the application on your device, then open it to configure. Make sure you have a Nintendo ID and have set up an account for yourself, as you will use it to control and set up your child's account. If you do not have a Nintendo ID, follow the link below to create a Nintendo account. Installing the application allows you to set times for access and control the Switch from afar. If you own a Switch, installing this application is recommended.

Nintendo ID Creation Link: https://accounts.nintendo.com/login?post_login_redirect_uri=https%3A%2F%2Faccounts.nintendo.com%2F

Nintendo 3DS

Many children have Nintendo's 3DS. While there are numerous versions, this guide should work for most of them. Before setting up parental controls, make sure the 3DS is updated to the latest version, and you have created your account, which you will use to lock down your child's account. If you have a Nintendo Wii U or Switch, you already have a Nintendo ID, which you can link to the 3DS. If you need to create your user account, and do not have a Nintendo ID, follow the instructions below:

1. Select "System Settings" from the Home Menu.
2. Select "Nintendo Network ID Settings," then "OK."
3. Read the information, then select "Next."
4. Select "Create a New ID," then select "Next."
5. You will be prompted to create a "Mii," if you do not have one. Create one; it does not matter how it looks; you can change it later if you wish.
6. Read through the information, then select "Understood" to continue.
7. Click "View the Network Services Agreement."
8. Select a language.
9. Read through the Network Services Agreement, then select "I Accept" to continue.
10. Enter the following information: Birthdate, Gender, Country of Residence, Region, and Time Zone.
11. You will now create a Nintendo ID. Be careful; you cannot change the ID once created.
12. Now, create a password for your Nintendo ID, then select "Confirm."
13. Enter the password again to verify, then select "Confirm."
14. Now, enter your e-mail address. Select "Confirm."
15. Enter the e-mail address again to verify, then select "Done."
16. Once you have filled out all fields, select "Done."
17. Review the information and make sure it is correct. Select "Link" to confirm.
18. Verify if you would like to receive promotional e-mails from Nintendo.
19. Verify if you would like to access Nintendo Network services from other devices.
20. Select "OK" to complete the process.
21. An e-mail will be sent to your address. Follow the instructions to verify and complete your account creation.

Once you have a user account, you can set up Parental Controls. To do so, follow the instructions below:

1. From the Home Menu, select "System Settings."
2. Select Parental Controls, then press "Yes."
3. It will ask the following: "Do you want to configure these settings now?'. Choose, "Yes."
4. Select "Next."
5. Read the following information, then tap "OK."
6. Tap "OK" again, then select a four-digit PIN. Make sure you pick a PIN you will remember that your child will not be able to guess. You will enter the PIN twice.
7. Now, you will create a Secret Question. You can choose to use a predefined question or make your own. Make sure your children cannot guess the answer to your question. Also, any answer to the question is case sensitive.
8. Follow on-screen prompts until it asks you, "Please consider registering an e-mail address." Go ahead and do so, this way in case you use your PIN, you can reset it via e-mail. Make sure your child does not have access to your e-mail address. Follow on-screen prompts until it asks for you to input your e-mail address. You will be required to input your e-mail address twice to confirm.
9. Once your e-mail address is confirmed, you will be able to select which items you wish to restrict.

Now that you have access to their 3DS, you will be able to go item by item and restrict access. Again, if you are unfamiliar with a game or application, conduct a Google search to learn more.

Internet Access / Router

For most devices beyond cell phones, your home Internet is the heart of your electronics. Without the Internet, most games and applications will be limited or non-functional. You need to take control over your home network, so you can limit or shut it down if needed.

Most home networks use a Router to send the Internet throughout your home. A Router will create a wireless network which often requires a password to access. If a device does not have the password, it will not be able to connect. One way of limiting access to the Internet is to change this wireless password, so your child does not have access to it.

Most Routers will allow you to change the Wireless Network Key. Do note, once you change the Wireless Network Key on the Router, you will need to update each device with the new key to have access.

Some Routers have a button called WPS. WPS stands for Wi-Fi Protected Setup. If WPS is enabled, it will allow a device to easily connect to the network, even if you do not have the key. If you are going to change keys to limit access, you will need to disable the WPS button, as your child may be able to reconnect by pressing this button then reconnecting their device. Many Routers allow this button to be disabled in their settings.

There are thousands of Routers and network configurations, making a guide on setting these up impossible. To set up your Router, look on the back and find its model number. If your Router is provided by your cable or phone company, contacting them and asking how to access your Router is a good step.

Once you have a model number, search for it in Google. You will need a Username and Password. Often these are factory defined values. If you cannot find the Username and Password for the Router on Google, contact the Router manufacturer and ask. Once you have a Username and Password, you can log in and begin configuring.

WARNING: Be careful what you change in your Router configuration! You could break it if you do not know what you are doing. Many of the settings are for professionals. If you have never configured a Router before, you may want to let an expert do so for you, or at least call your Internet provider and ask for assistance. If you do something that breaks your Router, most of them have a small pinhole that you can press that resets them to factory settings. Make sure you do your research on your Router before completing this step.

Today's Activity

For the next three days, begin enabling parental controls for all electronics in your home. Likely, this guide did not cover all the devices you own. For those, conduct Google searches to learn more about how to enable parental controls. Also, the information in this guide may be out of date. If these instructions do not work, conduct a Google search to assist you.

It may take some time for you to enable parental controls on all your devices. If it takes more than three days, that is fine. Before you continue with this book, be sure all devices are locked down as much as possible.

For most of these devices, you will not be able to set limits on usage time. You will need to continuing monitoring time using RescueTime or your logbook. Hopefully, in the contract you made with your family, you have created set times for access. If not, you will revise the contract together as a family towards the end of the book.

Your child may be upset with these changes and feel it is an invasion of privacy. Feelings such as these are normal and expected. If your child resists, explain to them your reasons, mainly that of safety. Have a conversation with your child, and invite your child to be present when you enable parental controls so that they will have input. Just make sure they do not see what PIN or password you put in. Always involve your child in these processes, and allow them to provide input. Talk to your child about this step first, then begin enabling parental controls on their devices.

Quick To-Do List

1. Talk to your child about setting up Parental Controls on all electronic devices, then start configuring on all personal computers, gaming consoles, phones, tablets, and finally, your Router. Make sure all children have these limitations, not just the one addicted to electronics.

Tomorrow's Focus

These next three days will likely be difficult as you finish locking down your child's devices. Tomorrow, you will begin focusing on your child's sleep, as they are most likely sleep deprived. Continue monitoring your child's electronic usage, as well as practicing coping skills, as these coping skills will be needed soon.

DAY 17: DAILY ROUTINE - SLEEP

One of the most important things you can do to improve your child's life is to ensure they get enough sleep. We often underestimate the importance of sleep, feeling it is something we can forgo at a whim. Research has found sleep is a critical component of physical and mental health, in particular for children.

Unfortunately, your child may be sleep deprived because of their addiction to electronics. Many children wake up at least once a night to check social media or to watch a video. It is time to make changes that will allow your child to sleep better, which means removing electronics from their rooms at night.

Removing Electronics From Their Bedroom

As phones, tablets, and computers have most likely become a distraction at night, it is time to remove them from your child's room. Remove all electronics from their bedroom, including computers, tablets, gaming consuls, portable gaming devices, and phones. Unplug their electronics, including chargers, and move them into your bedroom. Hopefully, you have already addressed this in the contract.

Your child will likely resist this move and become upset. They will not understand why they cannot have phones in their rooms, citing their friend's lack of restrictions. One way around this is to give them access to phones or tablets at specific times, then collecting them once the time is up. Specifying electronic access in the contract is a good idea. For example, you may have a rule in the contract as follows:

"No electronics, including phones, tablets, or gaming consoles, will be in children's rooms past 9:00 PM on school nights, and 11:00 PM on weekends".

For televisions, you can collect the power cord each night if you want to limit access. I highly recommend limiting television access, as your child may gravitate towards television if they do not have their tablet or cell phone. Creating a rule covering television in the contract is a good idea. Adjust these rules for each child based on age. Older children will not have the same access times as younger children. Set these rules in the contract, and make sure to enforce it.

As parents, you need to limit your access as well, so you can be an example. Past a certain time, you need to limit your access, as you need to sleep. Let your children know your limitations, so they will not feel singled out.

Today's Activity

For today's activity, besides removing all electronics from your child's room, you are going to create a routine, a habit, of when your child wakes up in the morning and he or she goes to sleep. You need to make sure they get at least eight hours of sleep, as they are most likely sleep deprived and may require more than average. You need to pick a time for them to sleep each night and a time to wake up each morning. For the rest of your time in this book, your child will adhere to this routine each day.

On weekends, try to keep the times similar to the school week. If your child gets up at 6:00 AM for school, getting up at 10:00 AM on the weekend is too much of a gap. Have them get up at 7:00 or 7:30 instead. You may need to change your sleeping schedule to match your child, so you can make sure they follow it. You will have to sacrifice some of your routines to make sure your child is following theirs. However, this will also help you, as you may need more sleep.

Today, create a routine for each child and each parent and place it in the contract. Note weekends, school days, and holidays and record times for them as well. Sometimes there will be variance in their routine, which is to be expected. However, try to stick with this routine for at least five days out of the week.

If your child uses their phone as an alarm clock, you will need to purchase an alarm clock, as their phone will no longer be in their room. Do so, then help them configure it. They will need to remember to set it each day, but this will help teach responsibility and foster the routine. Buy an old-fashioned alarm clock, one with no access to the Internet. Have your child use the alarm clock daily to adjust to their new sleeping schedule.

Quick To-Do List

1. Remove all electronics from your child's room, especially phones, tablets, and computers. Make sure to remove all electronic chargers as well.
2. Create a new sleep schedule for your child, making sure it is for 8–9 hours a night. Have them follow this schedule daily for the rest of the book.
3. Buy an alarm clock for your child if they do not already have one, and have them use it for now on.

Tomorrow's Focus

With their room free of electronics, over time, your child's sleep will improve. At first, you may not notice much of a difference, as they will need time to adjust to the change. However, over time they will sleep more throughout the night and will be healthier. Tomorrow, you will begin finding alternative activities for electronics, such as new hobbies or social activities, for your child. Over time, you will help your child discover different hobbies that can take the place of electronics.

DAY 18: NON-ELECTRONIC ACTIVITIES

S hortly, you will remove access to many of the applications and activities your child uses daily. While your child will have time at home for these activities, they will be without them during much of the day. During this period, they will become bored and fight you for access. It is time to find alternative activities, ones that do not require electronics.

Finding non-electronic activities will be difficult, as much of our entertainment is online. From TV shows to games, to music, to reading, everything is now online. It will take work, and creativity, to find real-world activities that can replace electronic ones. To do so, you will first revisit the list of Needs you created on Day's 10 and 11 to help you find activities to match their Needs.

Needs Revisited

Take the list of Needs you made on Day 10 and 11. Do you notice a pattern? From this list, you should get an idea of why your child spends so much time online. For many children, it is about social interaction and feelings of control. A child who spends much of her time on social media, for example, may use these applications to supply her Need for Acceptance or Inclusion. Another child who plays online games may satisfy his Needs for Choice and Community.

Your child needs real-world activities that correspond to their Needs. If your child has Needs to connect with others, then real-world activities that are social in nature are recommended. If your child plays video games due to the challenge, find real-world activities that stimulate a challenge.

Today's Activity

Today, you will make a list of real-world activities that you can introduce to your child. A good list includes activities the child can do alone and others they can do with a group. Social interaction is important for children, especially teenagers.

Below is a list of real-world activities you can use as a sample. Go through this list, then write down items that may interest your child. Feel free to add any items not on this list on yours:

- Astronomy.
- Board Games (Including Table Top Games or Card Games).
- Camping.
- Collecting (Rocks, Coins, or any real-world object).
- Cooking (including Baking and Grilling).
- Dancing.
- Drawing.
- Engineering (Building a model, robot, or something mechanical).
- Fashion Design.
- Fishing.
- Gardening.
- Hunting (With a parent or other adult).
- Meditation.
- Model Crafting.
- Music (Listening, Playing, or Composing).
- Painting.
- Photography.
- Playing Sports (Non-Professional or School-Based).
- Reading.
- Skateboarding (With proper safety equipment + training).

- Writing.
- Working Out.
- Yoga.

The list above contains a good mix of activities your child can do alone and with others. When making your list, choose at least three activities you could see your child liking. Tonight, sit down with your child and go over this list, asking them what they think, and if they have any ideas. Activities can have some online components, but make sure the activity is mainly something non-electronic.

Once they have chosen three hobbies, I suggest you begin researching how to start them. Weekends are great times to try new hobbies. Your next Family Day, for example, could include one of these activities. Your child does not have to like the activity or hobby, but they need to try. You may need to try many different hobbies before they find one that they enjoy.

Meetup.com

Once you have found a hobby your child enjoys, I recommended adding social interaction. One way you can do this is by attending a meetup.com group with your child. Meetup.com is a website where people schedule groups, weekly or monthly, where people meet at a location in the real world. Each group specifically focuses on an activity or a topic. For large geographical areas, you can find groups covering thousands of different activities. Below is a list of meetup.com's main categories:

Outdoors & Adventure

Tech

Family

Health & Wellness

Sports & Fitness

Learning

Photography

Food & Drink

Writing

Language & Culture

Music

Movements

LGBTQ

Film

Sci-Fi & Games

Beliefs

Arts

Book Clubs

Dance

Pets

Hobbies & Crafts

Fashion & Beauty

Social

Career & Business

Each category has numerous groups to join. Joining is free, and you can even create a group in your area if one does not exist for a particular activity. Once your child has committed to an activity, search meetup.com, and see if a group exists in the area for their age group. If so, have your child attend, making sure you are present, so your child is safe. Do some research ahead of time before attending the group.

Quick To-Do List

1. Take your child's List of Needs, and from it, make a list of activates they may enjoy. Talk with your child and have them pick three activities they would like to try.
2. Within the next few weeks, begin these activities with your child as alternatives to electronic activities.

3. Once your child has committed to an activity, look for a meetup.com group in your area for this activity. Make sure to research this group and attend the group with your child, so they are safe.

Tomorrow's Focus

It may take a month or two for your child to find real-world hobbies they enjoy. Even though they may resist, over time, they will have a healthier balance of activities. Tomorrow, you will schedule another Family Day, so your family can spend more time together. Continue to practice meditation, equal breathing, and grounding techniques, as you and your child will need them in the days ahead.

DAY 19: FAMILY DAY

Today is an easy day, after all the work you have done during the past week. Today, you will schedule another meeting with your family to discuss something fun to do together.

Try to remember who picked the family activity you did last time, so another member of your family can choose. If it came to a popular vote, do so again, making sure each person has a say.

Today's Activity

Schedule your meeting, making sure to pick a place that allows for family interaction. You can use the list of activities yesterday, as well as the list below, for ideas:

- Go to an observatory.
- Attend a play or poetry reading.
- Go to the library.
- Attend a festival.
- Go camping.
- Attend a concert.

If you need help thinking of ideas, look in your local newspaper to see what events are happening in your area. Sometimes you can find interesting events not advertised on TV. Get a list of ideas, and ask your children to think of some as well. Pick your activity, and have fun.

Quick To-Do List

1. Conduct another family meeting, discussing something you can do for fun. Make sure your children are involved in choosing the activity. Once you have picked your activity, go and do it shortly.

Tomorrow's Focus

Hopefully, you will have picked something you and your family are anticipating. Spending time with your family and having fun is vital for this process. Tomorrow, you will begin limiting your child's access to electronics on a case by case basis. You will use the list of their most addictive apps you created on Day 7 and began removing these apps from mobile devices. Continue using your coping skills daily, and make sure your child is following their new sleep schedule.

DAY 20: LIMITING ACCESS PART 1

T oday is going to be a stressful day. I am not going to sugar coat it. Today, you are going to begin limiting your child's access to the Internet. To do so, you will remove access to two of the activities on the list of addictive applications you made on Day 7. By removing access to these applications on mobile devices, you can be in control of when and where your child accesses them.

You will allow access to these applications on a PC or device that stays in the home. The goal is for your child not to be tempted by these applications in the real world. For example, if your child is consistently on Snapchat, they are likely not paying attention in school. By removing Snapchat from their phone, they will be less distracted. Before you begin removing applications, make sure you have locked down your child's device and have prevented them from installing applications. Review Days 14 through 16 if you have not done so.

Reviewing the Data

Days ago, you were asked to monitor all your child's time online. You listed the five most time-consuming activities and averaged the times. Today, you will review RescueTime or the log you created, and determine if these applications are the same. If so, then you know the applications you will need to limit going forward. If not, adjust your list. During the remainder of this book, you will continue to monitor your child's time online, so you can know if these changes are working.

Your list of applications can include examples such as Twitter, Facebook, Snapchat, or games, such as Farmville, Team Fortress 2, or League of Legends. Once you have your list, you are going to limit access to the least time-consuming applications.

Cutting Access

You are going to remove activity #5 and #4 from all portable devices. For example, if Twitter and Facebook are #5 and #4 on your list, you will remove the applications from your child's phone, or you will disable them if you cannot delete them. Your child will no longer have access to these two applications during the day.

Your child can have access to these applications during their electronics time in the evenings. Hopefully, you specified in their contract this time, and are abiding by it. Make sure you spell out consequences for using these applications at other times and be sure to enforce them.

Why Not Limit Their Most Time-Consuming Activity?

It may make more sense to begin to limit the most time-consuming activity on their list. However, this would most likely lead to conflict, as your children are not accustomed to having limits placed on them. By removing their least addictive applications, they will learn how to manage their feelings once you limit their most time-consuming activity. Trying to limit all activities at once will lead to a conflict you may not win.

Your child will need time in this process to manage their feelings and learn how to exist with limits. They are going to resist. Try not to become emotional or lose control of your behavior when they refuse to comply. Remember, your children will push you to test your limits. If you cave or become overly emotional, they will have the upper hand.

Today's Activity

It is time to go to each portable device and remove the bottom two applications on their list. Make sure to delete the applications from ALL mobile devices. If your child has a sibling who uses this device, you may need to remove it as well. At times, your child will likely sneak access until they are used to these restrictions. Do not give up hope if this happens. Addicts are resourceful and will find ways to satisfy their cravings. However, over time, the steps you are taking will help them gain more control over their behavior.

Quick To-Do List

1. Take the list you made on Day 7 of your child's more addictive activities, then remove the bottom two applications from all mobile devices. Allow access to these applications at home, during their allotted electronics time.

Tomorrow's Focus

Today was likely a difficult day, as you may have struggled to remove these applications from your child's devices. Tomorrow you will conduct another family meeting, where you will give a status update on how things are going for your family, discussing the positives and things that need improvement. Continue monitoring your child's online time, as well as taking care of yourself.

DAY 21: THE FAMILY MEETING – PART 2

I n your opinion, how have things gone so far? Are you noticing any changes within your family? Do you see changes within yourself? You have spent at least 20 days working through this book and making changes. Some of these may have gone well; others likely have not. You have probably seen resistance and conflict, as many of these changes are difficult. Today, you will conduct another family meeting to discuss the accomplishments and challenges during this period.

Focus on Accomplishments

During this meeting, focus on the accomplishments your children have experienced during this process. If your child is abiding by the contract, praise them by telling them how well they are doing. For example, if your daughter has spent more time with friends instead of spending time on social media, praise her for it.

During this process, your children need positive reinforcement. Telling your child he or she has done well will help build their confidence and self-esteem. Each day you need to praise them for things, even if they are small. If your child struggles with school, then makes a good grade on a quiz, praise them. Without your positive reinforcement from you, they will find their own, which may be in electronics or games. Ask each member of your family about their accomplishments, from their viewpoint, as well as the challenges they have faced as of late. You want to learn how they feel during this process, so they can see you value their opinions.

Include Yourself

In the meeting, make sure to discuss your challenges and accomplishments. Discuss ways you have had to change how you interact with technology and any struggles you have faced. If you have had to struggle with limiting your electronic usage at night, tell them of your struggle. They need to know this is not easy for you, and that you have had to make changes too.

Today's Activity

Conduct the family meeting, focusing on each child's accomplishments, strengths, and challenges. Continue to talk with them about what they are doing well while also discussing their challenges. Do the same for yourself and any adult in the family. All members of the family must take part in the family meeting. Until you have conducted the family meeting, do not continue past this chapter in the book. Keep practicing coping skills and monitoring your child's online time.

Quick To-Do List

1. Conduct a family meeting focusing on successes and challenges while working through this book. Make sure to include all members of the family, including the adult members of the family.

Tomorrow's Focus

With the family meeting concluded, you have learned more about what each of your family members thinks about their progress. Resistance will continue. While I sound like a broken record, this process will take time, and your children will fight you from making these changes. No family meeting is going to be rainbows and sunshine. Everything you do in this process is a learning experience for them and yourself.

Tomorrow, you are going to continue limiting your child's online access. You will remove the third activity from their list of most addictive applications you make on Day 7. Also, you are going to limit what your family does on their mobile devices while in public. You will be the model in this, by limiting what you do with your mobile devices while in public, then teaching them to do the same. Continue practicing your coping skills, and take time for yourself. You have done well so far; keep it up!

DAY 22: LIMITING ACCESS PART 2

Answer this, how often do you bring out your phone in public? Is it once an hour or once every 10 minutes? When you bring out your phone, do you even realize it, or is it an automatic process? How often does your spouse, significant other, or children criticize you for being on your phone?

Many people with smartphones are becoming dependent on them, reaching levels of addiction. There is a new anxiety called "Fear Of Missing Out," which some mental health professionals want to classify as a real anxiety disorder. As more and more people are using smartphones and becoming dependent, Fear Of Missing Out could become a legitimate disorder.

If you have had problems managing your screen time, imagine the struggle your children face, who do not have an adult's brain development or experience. In truth, we have no idea of the long-term impact of screen time, as it is so new.

Today, you are going to remove the 3rd most addictive application from your child's mobile devices, as well as begin setting rules for phones and tablets in public. You are going to make these changes first as a model for your family.

Your Phone is Distracting You From Life

Answer this: do you browse your phone when you are eating? How about while you are driving? How about when you are watching a television program or having a conversation with a coworker? Most likely, the answer to most of these questions is yes.

It is not just you; it is all of us. I have to watch my phone usage and sometimes find it difficult not to check my phone in the middle of a conversation, or when I am driving down the freeway. We are so used to this behavior; we no longer notice when we do it.

The problem, again, is with communication and social relationships. If you are on your phone during a conversation, you are telling the person you are speaking with that they are not worth your undivided attention.

Take Control of your Phone

You're going to begin to take notice of when you check your phone and when you keep it away. Below is a list of places where you will keep your phone in your pocket, purse, or someplace out of sight:

- While eating, especially out in public with people.
- While you are walking down the street.
- While in a shopping mall, store, or other retail establishments.
- While you drive.
- While at work (unless you use your phone for work).
- While at school (unless you use your phone for school).

In each location, keep your phone out of sight and focus on the environment. Use the phone only if needed. Addiction aside, many people are hurt or killed by not paying attention to their surroundings by being on their phones. While this may seem like common sense, most people use their phones in public and put themselves at risk of being robbed or hurt.

Today's Activity

Today, you will inform your family members of these limitations with smartphones, and you are going to tell them it applies to you first. You want to let them know that this will likely be a struggle for you, but that you are up to the challenge. You want them to know that they will soon follow these rules, but you will first be the model.

Also, today you will go to each of your child's portable devices and delete their 3rd most used application. Make sure to remove this application from all mobile devices, not just cell phones. Your child can use these applications at home during their allotted electronics time, but they will not in school or other public places.

You will also keep your cell phone out of sight while you are in public by keeping your phone in a purse, pocket, or bag. While you are driving, I suggest you keep your phone in the trunk or glove compartment, especially if you often check your phone while you drive. You can be out of touch with the world for a while. It is not worth getting killed or killing someone else. Keeping all phones out of reach is a good way for families to talk and communicate with each other.

Don't forget to use your coping skills, as anxiety may be high. The coping skills utilized in this book are not just for your child but for you. Taking care of yourself is a priority.

Quick To-Do List

1. Remove your child's 3rd most used application from their portable devices, giving them access to this application during their electronics time at home.

97

2. While in public, or driving, or eating, keep your cell phone out of sight, so you can begin to control your usage. You will model this behavior, which later will be for all members of the family.

Tomorrow's Focus

Tomorrow is all about you. You have spent time making changes for your child and your family. We are going to focus on you and your well-being and health. As a parent, you need to take care of yourself and your needs. For the next two days, you will focus mostly on you, your health, and your thoughts. You will learn how to think more positively and will be better able to meet the challenges of your child's addiction. For the next two days, the work is yours.

DAY 23: PERSONAL REFLECTION

H ow are you doing, really? Are you sleeping well? How is your anxiety? Is your mood stable, or does it vary widely during the day? These questions are important, as you need to begin making changes for your health.

At the beginning of this book, we talked about you and your addictions, challenges, and overall health. We will revisit each of these areas as a way to check in on your progress. Once this day is complete, you will have a homework assignment of your own.

Your Health

While working through this book, have you noticed any health changes? Are you getting enough sleep, or are you worried about your child and family late at night? How is your diet? Are you eating well, or are you too stressed to cook?

While these questions may seem straightforward, their impact is not. As you are working to improve your child's life and health, so too must you improve yours. Are you limiting time at night with electronics, and if so, has this improved your sleep? Have you set a sleep and wake schedule for yourself, as you have done with your child?

How are your stress levels? Do you have high levels of anxiety on most days?

If so, you need to practice and use the coping skills from Chapter 12. I know, grounding, meditation, and equal breathing sound strange and weird, but they work with time and practice. Most parents struggle with learning these coping skills, which in turn means their child struggles. It would help if you practiced them so that you can reduce anxiety and stress in your life.

Your Addictions

If you have any addictions, how have you done to fight them while working in this book? It does not matter what the addiction is, from electronics to sugar to alcohol; addiction is addiction. You need to be invested in fighting these addictions, just as much as you are in fighting your child's addiction.

Have you gotten help for them? Are there any support groups in your area? Have you seen a therapist for help in treating these addictions? One of the most important things you can do while working through this book is to see a therapist for your child and yourself. You need just as much therapy as your child in dealing with your child's addiction, not to mention your own. I recommend finding a therapist for your child and yourself.

Your Challenges

While working through this book, what challenges have you faced? For some, it will be the Family Meetings, with the conflict and resistance. For others, it will be Family Days, where you, as a parent, see your child check out and be miserable. Others, it is the limit setting and monitoring of your child. Be honest in the assessment of your challenges, as challenges are common and frequent.

At this point, you may not have noticed much progress and are losing hope. You may have expected 23 days into this book; you would have seen more progress. In truth, even limited progress is significant at this stage. Your family's problems go back years, and it will take months of work to repair them. For each activity or event that is positive, enjoy them. You are running a race, and right now, you have not even completed the first lap.

Your Accomplishments

What has gone well in the past three weeks? What accomplishments have you had at home, at work, or in your personal life? Like your child, you need to note your accomplishments and feel good about them. There is no shame in feeling good about something or enjoying yourself.

If you are having a difficult time thinking about accomplishments, focus, and spend time on them. Some people may resist feeling good about them, as they may feel this is prideful. A modest level of pride in oneself is healthy and needed. Reflect on accomplishments, even small ones, and feel good about them.

Your Homework

Today, you are going to begin something you may have never done before. For now on, you are going to undergo a daily activity designed to release stress while also cataloging your experiences. Today, you will begin the process of journaling, so you have a record of your thoughts and experiences. This journal will be a reference point when you look back at your experiences with this book.

Fortunately, journaling is not a challenging activity. A useful journal is one that is brief, honest, and completed often. You are writing this journal for yourself, designed for you to read and learn from at a later date. You have nothing to prove, and no one else should ever read it. Journaling is a private experience you only share with yourself. Journaling is a form of release and is a way to get out feelings or thoughts you cannot otherwise.

Journaling: An Example

So, what makes a good journal entry? Below is a sample journal entry of someone working through this book:

"May 9th, 2017

Today was rough. Jonny refused to get off his DS before dinner again. I reminded him of the contract and told him he had used his two hours, but he ignored me. I took away the DS, with him yelling and screaming at me. I was calm and told him the rules, and told him he could have it back tomorrow if he behaves. I felt like a bad parent with my child yelling at me like that.

I just want to break this DS in half and throw away all electronics! I get so pissed this is happening to my family. I am working to control my anger, but sometimes it slips out. I felt hopeless tonight and drank. I know I am drinking too much, but it is one of the things that helps me calm down. I see my therapist tomorrow, and I know I gotta tell her about my drinking. This is so hard, and sometimes I do not see the light at the end of the tunnel. Tomorrow I will see my therapist and tell her about my struggles, which will help. I can make changes, I will make changes, but sometimes it is so hard. For myself and my child, I will try".

The overall theme of this entry is honesty. In it, the author feels overwhelmed with the struggle of their child's addiction to electronics. So much so, the author is drinking to cope with the stress. By writing these thoughts down, they are no longer bottled up inside. No one will read the journal; it is a form of release. The author decides to tell their therapist about their drinking and ends the entry with hope for the future.

The main rule of journaling is being honest with what you write. If you are angry, write you are angry. If you feel hopeless, write you feel hopeless. Do not exaggerate or reduce the impact of your emotions. Be real and honest, and let it out. Journaling is one of the best coping skills in dealing with stress.

Today's Activity

Today, begin your journal writing exercise. I want you to write about 1-2 paragraphs a day. Do not focus on grammar or spelling, as this is for your eyes only. Be honest about today and write about your experiences. Include problems you had at work, or school, or with people. Discuss your feelings and reactions to these problems. Write about your child, their addiction, and any family problems you are currently experiencing. Write about your addictions or problems as well. Journaling is a powerful exercise in letting go of past feelings and regrets. I want you to journal every day, even once you have finished this book.

Quick To-Do List

1. Begin a daily journal, and keep writing in it each day. Focus on yourself, your child, and your family in this journal. Be honest in it, as it is for your eyes only.

Tomorrow's Focus

Tomorrow, you begin to change the way you think about your child's addiction, yourself, and your family. You will begin to learn how to manage negative thoughts, from guilt to predicting the future. By learning how to combat negative thoughts, you will be in a better state of mind and will be better equipped to deal with your child's addiction to electronics. Begin your journal tonight, as you will need it in the days ahead.

DAY 24: AUTOMATIC NEGATIVE THOUGHTS

T oday is an important day, as you will begin to learn more about what controls your thoughts. Controlling your thoughts is not a simple task, as our thoughts are often chaotic and negative. Today, you will learn what goes into our thoughts and how we can better control them and our behaviors. By learning to control your thoughts better, your relationship with your child and family will improve.

Are All Thoughts True?

How often do you think your brain lies to you? When a thought comes to mind, does it have to be true, or can it be an impulse? If our brains lie to us, then how do we know what is true? These are all good questions, as our brains are incredibly complex. Your brain is completing thousands of actions a second, often without your knowledge or input.

The problem begins with conscious thought. As humans, we are wired to notice threats to our lives. In the past, if we were not on the lookout for danger, we would have been eaten or killed. As a result, our brains have adapted to look for danger in all forms; the more threats we notice, the greater the chances of staying alive.

What do threats have to do with thoughts? Threats are often negative thoughts used to seek out problems. If we feel something is a threat, our anxiety levels rise, which allows us to be more alert and able to act. Negative thoughts, in a way, are a type of survival skill. Negative thoughts can help us be more alert and adaptive.

The problem is, over time, we rely on negative thoughts too much and begin to believe them as truth. Sometimes, our brains lie to us as a way to protect us from something unpleasant. For example, if I have social anxiety, I have a fear of interacting with others. My brain tells me people are not to be trusted so that I can avoid this fear. This lie protects me from pain, even though it is false. Our brains lie to us in an attempt to shelter us from painful experiences. Over time, however, these thoughts become poisonous and prevent us from living life.

Automatic Negative Thoughts

Everyone has negative thoughts. If someone tells you they never have negative thoughts, they are lying. Everyone has negative thoughts, often hundreds of times daily. The term, Automatic Negative Thoughts, is a way to explain our thoughts and how they work. Automatic means, well, automatic. These thoughts come without choice.

You may be thinking; if automatic negative thoughts always happen, then I am doomed to failure. False! You cannot control negative thoughts from appearing in your mind, but you can control how you **respond** to them.

For example, if you had social anxiety and thought of going out in public, you may have the following thought: "Everyone is going to look at me and judge me!". This thought would be automatic, appearing in your mind. You can now choose to believe this thought, allowing it to influence your actions, or you can challenge the thought as false. At this point, you are in control and can choose to believe the thought as truth or a lie. Automatic negative thoughts are often designed to limit our exposure to pain, causing more pain in the future.

Different Types of Automatic Negative Thoughts

An easy way to remember automatic negative thoughts is to use the word ANTS. Like real-life ants, automatic negative thoughts often sting and come in groups. One negative thought leads to many. I did not come up with the concept of ANTS; that honor belongs to Dr. Daniel G. Amen. Check out his work to learn more about controlling ANTS once you have finished this chapter.

Dr. Daniel G. Amen: https://danielamenmd.com/

Below is a list of the eight most common ANTS. Make no mistake, ANTS are your enemy, and to fight your enemy; you have to know them:

- All or Nothing Thinking – Thinking in terms of black and white or in extremes.
- Overgeneralization – Using words such as "always" and "never" directed at yourself.
- Filtering – Stripping the positives from a situation and focusing only on the negatives.
- Mind Reading – Thinking you know the thoughts of another when, in reality, you don't.
- Should Statements – Using the word "should" in a way to limit personal responsibility.
- Magnification – Thinking something is worse than it is.
- Guilt – Punishing yourself for past mistakes as excuses to continue your addiction.
- Predicting the future – Thinking you know the outcome of a situation when, in reality, you don't.

There is some overlap with this list, as many of these thoughts lead to the others. If you have seen these before, know ANTS are also known as cognitive distortions, with are often challenged in therapy. A therapist who practices Cognitive Behavioral Therapy knows ANTS well and can help you challenge negative thoughts.

Today, we are going to cover all the ANTS on this list. Once done, you will write down an example of the most common thought you experience for each ANT. You will begin to notice when you have these thoughts and learn how you can change them from negative to positive.

All or Nothing Thinking

With All or Nothing Thinking, thoughts are often extreme. Things are all good, or all bad, with no middle ground. This kind of thinking can leave one feeling depressed and angry. Anytime something happens that is even slightly negative, it is entirely bad, with no compromise.

For example, say your child woke up in the middle of the night and got on the Xbox One. He has done this before and is one of the things you are trying to prevent. You wake up hearing noises, and at 2:00 AM, you find him watching a YouTube video. You become furious and yell at him, telling him how he has disrespected you again. You begin thinking, "My child is lost, there is no hope," and go to bed, feeling upset and hopeless. The next day you are distant with your child, still angry, still feeling hopeless. When your child does well on a test at school, you do not show much enthusiasm, as you still feel they are lost.

In this example, even when the child does well, the parent is fixated on their child's failure the night before. This fixation continues over time until positives are ignored. This example is probably familiar to you, as you have likely been in this situation.

Reframing All or Nothing Thinking

Reframing is the process of challenging a negative thought, making it positive and more acceptable. Reframing is difficult as it needs to be done right as the thought forms. Waiting too long does not work, as one negative thought often leads to another, leaving the person overwhelmed.

To reframe a thought, first, note the type of thought and the feeling behind it. For the example above, the thought is: "My child refuses to change; there is no hope for the future." A feeling attached may be of disappointment, anger, both, or something else. Knowing the thought and the feeling begins the process of challenging the thought.

Once you know the feeling, you can step back and start to think about it rationally. Yes, your child snuck out at night to be on the Xbox, but is it the end of the world? It is one night out of thousands. How about the nights he did not sneak on his Xbox? Likely, there are more instances of good than bad. Focusing only on negative events will leave you miserable and hopeless.

Next, take the original negative thought and make it more positive. One example would be:

"I felt disappointed and angry; my child snuck to play his Xbox at night. However, he has been punished, and it is over. I will not let it be the end of the world. I will talk to him about why he snuck out in the first place, so maybe it does not happen again."

Notice the feeling included, as you can still feel angry or disappointed, but without the extremes.

Last, make a conscious choice to move on and focus on something else. Do not sit and obsess over the disappointment. Move on and do something else to distract yourself from the thought, such as a grounding technique. Often

ANTS repeat, meaning you will have to reframe more than once. If you work this process, you will notice you are not as upset and are more adaptable to situations.

For today's activity, write down a recent example of All or Nothing thinking. Note the thought and the feelings associated with it. Next, write out the thought in a more positive way. Finish by writing down what you did to distract yourself and move on from the thought.

Overgeneralization

Overgeneralization uses words such as "always" and "never" to describe yourself and your future. These thoughts are associated with future actions, such as getting a job, finding a relationship, or being happy. Overgeneralization is highly destructive, as it limits your ability to see hope in the future.

In truth, overgeneralizations are excuses to fail. By saying things will "never" be successful, we permit ourselves to quit. Overgeneralization steals our will to try and allows us to remain miserable.

Using the example from All or Nothing Thinking, one thought may be, "My child will never overcome his addiction to electronics. It is hopeless". This is a dangerous thought, as it begins the process of distancing you from your child. If you think the situation is hopeless, you will start to detach emotionally, instead of focusing your time and efforts elsewhere. Over time, you may stop trying to fix the problem, resulting in your child getting worse and your family breaking further.

The same can apply to "always." "My child will always be an addict; there is nothing I can do!" As with "never," change is denied, resulting in a self-fulfilling prophecy.

Reframing Overgeneralization Thoughts

Like in our example with All or Nothing Thoughts, reframing works in the same way. First, list the exact thought and the feelings that accompany it. Our feelings for the example above may be despair, frustration, or anger.

Next, take a step back and think about the thought. How do you know your child will always be an addict, or that they will never get over their addiction? You do not see the future, and cannot know what tomorrow will bring. You have to resist the temptation to give up, and instead, focus on what your child is doing right. By asking these questions, you begin to challenge the validity of the thought.

Now, restate the thought in a more positive light.

"I sometimes feel frustrated and angry over my child's electronic usage, but I will not give up, and I will do what I can to reconnect with my child."

Notice the feeling word and the actions that follow. This thought is much more positive, as it is realistic and notes change.

Now, distract yourself by using a coping skill and move on. In our example, reconnecting with your child and improving communication are ways to begin implementing change. Look at a recent example in your life, and reframe it as you did with All or Nothing Thinking.

Filtering

Filtering is the conscious act of denying a situation's positives while instead only focusing on the negatives. If this sounds like All or Nothing Thinking, you are correct, with the only difference is the conscious choice of denying positives. By stripping away the positive, only negative, depressing content remains.

For example, say your child has been addicted to video games for years. You have worked to combat this addiction, with limited results. Your child's teacher at school has recommended they take up computer programming, which your child does. Over the next few months, your child's grades improve as they spend much of their time programming a game. Your child is more sociable and is learning a real-world skill. However, as your child uses electronic devices to make this game, you are unhappy and refuse to see improvement, as you feel your child has shifted the addiction from playing games to creating them. Even though your child's grades have improved, and they are more social, you refuse to see the positives.

For many parents, improvement in grades and social interactions would be worth praise; however, when parents get locked into a negative mindset, they begin to filter and limit positives. Over time, only negatives are seen, causing problems for the parent and the child.

Reframing Filtering

Reframing filtering involves focusing on the positives, as well as the negatives. Removing the negatives is counterproductive, as you cannot fix a problem you ignore. Instead, focusing on both positives and negatives is a healthy mix. The reframed thought may be as follows:

"I am glad my child is learning a real-world skill and is doing better in school. However, sometimes I feel they spend too much time on electronics. I will help my child by showing them other activities, and giving them limits on screen time, even for creating games, while also encouraging their work and success".

Notice the positives were at the beginning of the reframed thought. When reframing filtered thoughts, focus on positives first, as it takes more effort to focus on positive thoughts. The thought did not end there, with concern over too much screen time. We do not want to remove the negative thought but acknowledge it. Go ahead and write down your recent example of filtering, and reframe it.

Mind Reading

Can you read minds? No? Then why do you assume you know someone's thoughts? The truth is, we all mind read, more often than we would care to admit. Mind reading is damaging, especially in relationships, when we make assumptions on how someone thinks. Mind reading can change how we act towards others, with devastating consequences.

For example, say you and your spouse have a 12-year-old son who plays Minecraft for 6-8 hours a day. You are not into video games and do not know much about them. On the other hand, your spouse has played games for years and introduced Minecraft to your son. You are concerned your child is becoming addicted to Minecraft, while in the past, your spouse has appeared less concerned. You have talked to your spouse about your son's screen time before, leading to an argument.

Over time, you begin assuming your spouse does not care about your son's screen time and believe he does not see playing games 6-8 hours a day as a problem. You begin thinking, "My spouse does not care; he refuses to see the truth." While you become angry over the issue, you are afraid to have a conversation, as you do not want a fight. You decide to limit your son's screen time, without consulting your spouse, which leads to a major fight. In the end, both your spouse and child are mad at you, and all you wanted was to lessen your son's screen time.

In this example, a lack of communication was the problem. We cannot read minds; we can only make assumptions. The assumptions above caused distance in the relationship, which in the end contributed to a major fight.

Reframing Mind Reading

When mind reading, do not automatically assume your thought is correct or incorrect. Treat it as a question you want to be answered. Sometimes thoughts can help us learn more about others, even though they may begin negatively. For our example, we will turn the thought into a question we can later answer with observation.

"Does my spouse think my son is spending too much time playing Minecraft? I don't know. He has never said so, all though he likes to play games. I need to talk with him, asking if he feels placing a limit on how much screen time our son has is needed at this time".

By reframing it into a question, you now have a choice. You can choose to find the answer or choose to ignore it. You can decide to talk to your spouse and raise your concerns over too much screen time, or you can ignore it and see what happens. By asking the question, you will not just assume the answer and will begin taking steps to solve it.

Imagine an instance lately where you were mind reading, and add it to your list, reframing as I have done above.

Should Statements

When was the last time you thought, "I should have ..." or, "he/she should have ... ". Should statements are problematic, as they are meaningless statements that add nothing of value to your life. Often I hear people tell me they "should" have done something. Or someone "should" have been nice to them. Both would be valid statements if we lived in a fair universe. Unfortunately, we do not. Life is not fair, period.

It would be great if we lived in a world where everyone was kind, considerate, and understanding to all around them. Instead, we live in a world with human beings who have flaws, faults, and problems. As a result, we say bad things because we have negative, bad thoughts. No amount of political correctness will change that. Should statements are bad, as they take us out of reality and give us excuses to fail.

Let us use the example for Mindreading, only this time, from the viewpoint of the spouse. You have noticed your son playing Minecraft 6-8 hours a day, and know you need to do something about it. You like Minecraft yourself, and at times you play together with your son. You have noticed you need to limit your screen time, but you do not want to, as it is your main hobby. You SHOULD limit your screen time, and your son's, but you feel it is not the right time. You think your spouse is becoming more upset over the issue, but you will wait until she brings it up.

By using the word should, we have no intention of following through. Most things we say we "should" do, we never do. We use this word to feel good about ourselves; by thinking we have a plan of action. In reality, we have a house of cards that will collapse on itself.

Reframing Should Statements

How then, do we say things correctly, if 'should' is a common part of our language? By reframing to a stronger, more command-driven word. For example:

*"I know I need to set limits on my son's screen time, and for myself, as well. I **will** talk with my spouse about this issue tonight, after dinner, to begin making a plan. Also, I **will** start thinking of alternatives to screen time, for myself and my son.".*

"**I will**" commands respect. It is a promise to yourself and others. Unless something happens that you cannot prevent, you will talk with your spouse and set limits for screen time. You have no trap door, no permission statement to avoid the situation. You will get it done!

At times you may have had problems completing assignments in this book. You may have thought you "should" monitor your child's screen time, or "should" have a Family Day, even though the last one did not go so well. We are all human and fall into this trap. For any activity you have not yet completed in this book, replace "should" with "will" and get it done. Think of an instance you used "should" lately and add it to your list.

Magnification

At times, we exaggerate our problems, especially to ourselves. We get so caught up in the moment we do not see the big picture. A small problem becomes enormous, costing us time and emotional energy. As we spend all our energy on small problems, we neglect the larger, more important ones. Magnification ANTS are common and painful.

There are thousands of possible examples to choose from to demonstrate magnification. A case in point would be your child's grades. While we want our children to do well, sometimes this will not happen. Sometimes it takes time to understand a new subject, and at times children fail. Sometimes they fail because they do not put enough effort in to succeed. For our example, assume your child has failed a major grade in Science due to not completing a project. Instead of completing the project, they played video games and lied about completing the project.

Being angry over the poor grade, as well as the lie, is normal and expected. Magnification comes in when we take things to the extreme. We begin having thoughts, such as "My child is just a liar and a failure. They will never succeed. All he wants to do is play games. He will never go to college or be successful like this".

These thoughts begin as anger but can end as hopelessness and despair. Yes, your child lied and misplaced his time; however, it is not the end of the world. It is one project out of hundreds. There need to be consequences for his actions, but taking things to extreme hurts your child and yourself.

Reframing Magnification

When a problem occurs, stop and take a deep breath, giving yourself time to think. Reframing the thought is not difficult if you give yourself time to do so. A possible reframed thought for the example above would look like this:

"I am angry right now for my son's failed project, and that he lied to me. He knew what he was doing, and will have consequences for this. However, it is just one project. I can use this as a learning experience for him, so he does not repeat his mistake".

Like our examples yesterday, begin reframing with the feeling you are experiencing. The goal is to admit your feelings, not bury them. Working with feelings lets them out, which makes keeping control of your emotions easier. By viewing the situation more positively, actions will be taken, such as letting this situation become a learning experience for your child. Write down an example of magnification you have experienced lately. Reframe your example like above.

Guilt

Guilt is a very nasty ANT and one of the worst on our list. Guilt is tricky, as it can have a positive purpose. When we do something wrong, guilt is our internal consequence. People without guilt are often manipulative, and some may be psychopathic. We all need healthy levels of guilt in our lives to help keep us in check.

The problem is when guilt becomes toxic. Over time, once we have learned from our mistakes, we need to let go and move on. Sometimes, depending on our mistakes' severity, we feel the need to continue to punish ourselves. Excessive guilt leads to a type of self-sabotage that, in the end, hurts us and others.

We all have had excessive guilt in the past. It is part of being human. The question is, why do we hold onto it, even if it hurts us? Earlier in the book, I made this statement: "**Everything we do helps us in the short-term, even if it harms us in the long term.**". In other words, this excessive guilt gives us some benefit, even as it hurts us.

How could excessive guilt benefit us? Excessive guilt permits us to fail by giving reasons not to try. Change is difficult, especially if one has a long, painful past. It is easy to say there is no hope and believe the problem is too great. Guilt gives us an excuse by telling us that we are bad people or that it is too difficult. This negative self-talk allows us to sit in our rut and do nothing.

For example, say in the past, you spent six years playing an online game, spending 12-14 hours a day. You have decided to quit, and over time you are successful. However, excessive guilt tells you that you ruined most of your life, that you will eventually relapse, and that you will never fully move past the addiction. You will always be a failure, and deep down, you have not recovered. The example above is a personal ANT I have to deal with daily. Guilt likes to tell me that I ruined my life when, in reality, I have used this period of my life to help others. You would not be reading this book if I had not experienced my addiction. I reframe this thought by giving evidence against it.

Reframing Guilt

It is time to stop living in the past, which is guilt's goal. The past is done, finished. You cannot change it. It is time to accept it and move on. When I get a guilt ANT, I reframe it as follows:

"While I mostly wasted six years of my life playing that game, I can use what I have learned to help others, which means I did not waste it after all. I have learned from it and now can manage my life".

Notice how I admit the thought is true. While I was addicted, I was wasting my life. But I have moved on. Now I have used the experience as motivation to help others. Therefore, there is nothing to feel guilty over; I have learned from it.

In the past, you may have experienced the following Guilt ANTS: "I have failed my child, as I did not get help for their addiction earlier." Or, "I got my child these gaming systems or cell phones, it is all my fault my child is an addict." It is time to forgive yourself, as you cannot see the future, and did not know your child would become addicted. If there is one activity I want you to do while working in this book, it is to forgive yourself for your mistakes and begin looking towards a future of action and change.

Guilt is an ANT you will have to reframe often, even for things long past. Now is the time to let the past go and focus on your future. Guilt is a thief that will steal your happiness if you let it.

I want you to write down the guilty thoughts you have had about you and your child's addiction. I want you to reframe them, as I have done above. I want you to reframe them every time they enter your mind.

Predicting the Future

For our last ANT on our list, we will choose one of the worst. While predicting the future, we make negative assumptions, leading to a lack of effort. Statements such as, "It's hopeless, I will never ..." and "Why try? It is hopeless," are negative and dangerous. By making negative assumptions about our future, we lose our will to try.

The truth is, the future is NOT set, and you have CONTROL in making it. You can choose to let your child's addiction win, or you can make sacrifices for your family to change. Predicting the future ANTs steal your ability to shape your future. If you believe the future is hopeless, then why try? Like guilt, predicting the future steals your motivation and hope.

The reverse can also be true when predicting the future in an unrealistically positive way. Statements such as "everything will always turn out right!" and "My child is fine, there will be no problems!" can lead to a lack of effort or preparation. Unrealistically predicting the future leads to denial of problems, which solves nothing. Focusing only on the positive is just as bad as only focusing on the negative.

Reframing Predicting the Future

First, stop and take a step back, and do not believe your lies. You do not know what the future holds, for if you did, you would play the lottery and be rich. None of us know what tomorrow will be. Would you want to? For me, knowing the future would rob me of free will, and I want to shape my future.

For example, if you think your child will always be an addict, here is how to reframe it:

"I refuse to believe my child will always be an addict. My child may have an addiction now, but I will work with them to fight it. In the end, I will choose my future and help my child choose theirs!".

Notice the direct attack toward "always"? Be specific and choose your thoughts carefully. Attack words such as never, always, and should. They attack you, so attack back! Do not give in to the lies of negative thoughts. Put some attitude in these thoughts! Make sure to focus on your future in these thoughts. You can add in a goal or something you want in the future that will motivate you.

Today's Activity

Congratulations, you just did it. By writing down your list of eight negative thoughts, complete with reframing, you have begun the process of challenging your thoughts. Learning to reframe your thoughts is a major step in fighting your child's addiction, as you will be more hopeful for the future.

Quick To-Do List

1. Complete your list of ANTS, including reframing, in your journal. Study this list often and memorize all the different ANTS.

Tomorrow's Focus

Learning to reframe your ANTS is vital for tomorrow's task. Tomorrow, you are going to remove the second most addictive application from your child's mobile devices. Study your list of ANTS, and do not forget to journal. Reframing ANTS in your journal is a good way to work through them.

DAY 25: LIMITING ACCESS PART 3

With less than a week left in this book, we have much to cover before you can take what you have learned and turn them into daily habits. Your goal is to continue these habits until they become second nature. Today, you are going to remove access to the second most time-consuming application from your child's phone and mobile devices.

A Recap

Hopefully, you have removed the bottom three applications from your child's mobile devices already. If you have not, do so today. These applications are time wasters that are distracting them from their life and responsibilities. Your child can use these applications during their electronics window based on the contract, but they need to focus on work, school, and relationships throughout their day.

If the list included game consoles or computer games, make sure to limit them at home. Often computer games and video games can be addictive, even more so than phone applications. Limiting time on these is just as critical as limiting your child's time on mobile games or social media.

Today's Activity

Right now, go ahead and remove the second application on your list from all your child's mobile devices. As with the other's, it should not take long. You may encounter more resistance from your child, as this activity is likely important to them. Talk with them about this action, and how important it is to limit their screen time. If they become angry or yell and scream, ignore it, and do not give in. Limiting their access to addictive applications is critical for them to gain control over their behaviors. Hold firm to your boundaries, and do not give in; your child's reaction is only temporary. Continue working with your child in finding new hobbies to replace their screen time. The more applications you remove, the more time they will have for new hobbies or activities.

Quick To-Do List

1. Remove the 2nd application on the list from all your child's mobile devices.

Tomorrow's Focus

You have learned much in the past few days. You know more about yourself, have learned how to reframe negative thoughts, and have limited many of the applications your child uses. Tomorrow, you will plan another Family Day, which will happen at least twice a month for now on. Make sure to continue practicing your coping skills, as well as journaling, where you can reframe negative thoughts you have had while removing your child's applications.

DAY 26: FAMILY DAY

With all the work you have done in the past week, you deserve a day of ease and relaxation. As you are the one that has done most of the work, today, you get to schedule a Family Day, making sure you choose something you want to do. The past Family Days have most likely focused on your children and what they have wanted to do. While you will ask their opinions, try to focus on a location you will enjoy.

Today's Activity

Schedule your meeting, making sure to pick a place that allows for family interaction. If you need help with thinking of ideas, below is a list of possibilities:

- Go to the beach.
- Go to the pool.
- Go to an observatory.
- Attend a play or poetry reading.
- Go to the library.
- Attend a festival.
- Go camping.
- Attend a concert.
- Go to the Park.
- Drive someplace new.
- Go to a Museum.

- Go to a Sporting Event.
- Go to the theater.
- Walk around the mall or some other large public place.
- Go to an amusement park.
- Go someplace different to eat.

One idea is to combine some of these activities. You could go to the pool in the morning, then go to an observatory at night. Be creative and think of activities you do not normally do with your family. There is nothing wrong with choosing things you would like to do as well. Have your meeting, and pick something you will enjoy.

Quick To-Do List

1. Conduct another family meeting, focusing on an activity you would enjoy, as well as your children. Once you have picked your activity, go and do it shortly.

Tomorrow's Focus

Have fun, and enjoy time with your family. While resistance may continue, your children will become used to spending time together as a family over time. Tomorrow, you finish removing your child's most addictive activity from mobile devices, which may cause the most resistance you have seen yet. Remember, their mobile devices are yours, as you likely purchased them, and are paying the bill to use them. Get a good night's sleep, and make sure your child continues to follow their sleeping schedule.

DAY 27: LIMITING ACCESS PART 4

oday may be the day you have dreaded for some time. If your child uses a mobile application as their primary activity, today will be difficult for them. They are used to having access to this application at all times and have likely become dependent on it. When removing this activity, understand their pain, fear, and loss, as they will probably be unequipped to handle this step without assistance from you. If your child sees a therapist, having their therapist involved in this process is recommended.

Use Your Coping Skills

Today you and your child will need all the coping skills they have learned so far. Hopefully, you have been practicing the coping skills learned in this book with your children as well as yourself. Meditating beforehand will help calm yourself down as you prepare for the conflict ahead. Use deep breathing and grounding during the process, especially if your child has a tantrum.

Today's Activity

It is time to remove the application from your child's mobile devices. Remember to combat any ANTS that may come up during this process. Reframe them, and do not let them stop you from completing the task. I suggest you remove the apps or activity in the following order:

1. Meditate for 15 minutes.

2. Gather all mobile devices.

3. Talk to your child about what you are going to do, making sure to be calm but firm.

4. Remove the application from all mobile devices.

5. Conduct a grounding exercise with yourself and your child if they are able.

6. Help your child engage in one of their new hobbies, diverting their attention away from the application you removed.

Removing the application is the first step; now, you will have to live with the consequences. Expect the next few days to be rough, as they will use their behavior as a way to express their anger towards you. This is a form of manipulation so that you will cave and return the applications. You may have experienced this already with the other applications you have removed.

No matter what happens, this is temporary. Over time your child will come to accept these limits. Eventually, your child will find other hobbies to replace these applications. Make sure you have removed the ability to reinstall applications on mobile devices, or you will find the application back on their mobile devices within an hour.

Your child may need space after this event. If so, let them have it. Give them time to adjust to this change. Make sure you are in control of your behavior and do not believe any ANTS that pop up. ANTS will be thick in your mind, telling you this will "never" work, and that your child will "always" hate you. These thoughts are lies, reframe these ANTS as you have learned, and continue.

Quick To-Do List

1. Using the order above, remove the final application from your child's mobile devices.

Tomorrow's Focus

Congratulations, you are nearly done with this book. You have made many changes in your child's life, your life, and the life of your family. Now, the real work begins, as you now have to maintain these changes for the foreseeable future.

Tomorrow, you will modify the Contract covering electronic devices for your family. You will modify it based on what you have learned so far. After tomorrow, you will focus on your child's career goals, then finish the book reflecting on what you have learned in this process. Enjoy the rest of the day; you have earned it.

PART 3: MAINTENANCE

DAY 28: THE CONTRACT – PART 2

A s you have worked through this book, you have likely observed changes that need to be made throughout your child's daily routine. You have removed electronics from their bedrooms, taught healthy coping skills, and limited access to electronics. Even with these changes, you have likely had ideas about improving your family's routine.

Today, you will take the Electronics Contract you created on Day 13 and will make these modifications. To do so, you need to evaluate what has worked and what has not. Not all the ideas in this book will work, as each family is different. It is time to make changes that best improve your family.

Individual Assessment

Later today, you are going to gather your family together and discuss the changes to the contract. Before you do, you will look over the contract with any other parents in the home, read over the contract, and propose changes.

For each item on the contract, evaluate how it has worked. Each item on the contract has likely had its challenges. Some have worked well, while others have not. What changes do you think will help? Maybe you are giving them too much time with electronics. Maybe you are not giving them enough. Maybe bedtime is too early, or too late? As parents, evaluate the contract and write down ideas on another piece of paper to discuss during the family meeting.

The Family Meeting

Next, gather your family together, making sure all members are present. Begin by discussing the successes of the contract. For each item your children have done well, praise them for it. Even if the items are small, your children need to know you appreciate their effort.

Next, discuss the challenges the parents have had while following the contract. If you have found it challenging to limit electronics usage in your bedroom, be honest, and discuss it. Let your children know they are not the only ones that are struggling with these changes.

Continue by discussing the challenges you have noticed with your children. You will likely encounter resistance, as they will minimize their failures or cite how the rule is "unfair." Let them know you hear their frustration and discuss with them what alternative ideas they may have. It is a good idea to have your children propose changes to the contract, so they can feel they have a voice. While you cannot agree with all their ideas, agreeing to some is a good balance.

Next, discuss the changes you have come up with during your assessment of the contract. Listen to your children and see what they have to say. Some of these ideas they may agree with, others they may fight. After discussing all these changes with the family, modify the contract for all children and parents.

Once the meeting is finished, finalize the contract and print it out, and post it in a public place. I recommend each month you gather as a family to discuss the contract and make adjustments.

Today's Activity

Conduct the family meeting and make changes to the contract. It is important to listen to your children, as they need to feel included in this process. Once you have finished with the contract, evaluate it through the next month to see if you need to make further changes. Over the next few months, your children will become used to this routine.

Quick To-Do List

1. Follow the daily routine you have created, making sure you complete it daily. Make adjustments when necessary.

Tomorrow's Focus

It is time to begin thinking of your child's future. For many children, thinking of a career and independence is frightening. This fear can linger from adolescence into adulthood, paralyzing them into inaction. Tomorrow, you will meet with your child and begin discussing what they want for the future, so they can start making a plan.

DAY 29: YOUR CHILD'S CAREER GOALS

I f your child is a teenager or will be soon, it is time to begin planning for their future. While most children will change their minds about what they want to do, it is important to think about the possibilities.

Most teenagers have ideas as to what they want to do but have not thought of specifics. Some have a general idea of a career they would find interesting but have never thought of what it takes to achieve it. It is time to begin researching these specifics, so your child can start to focus on what they need to learn to be ready.

Sadly, for many teenagers, the future looks bleak. They see a world with economic uncertainty, rising college costs, and an unstable workforce. With thousands of possible careers, teenagers often feel overwhelmed with the choices available to them. These worries can lead to a fear of the future, with electronics addiction as the coping skill of choice.

A Future of Fear

Many of my teenagers and young adults suffering from Internet Addiction have told me they are afraid of the future and of making a wrong career choice. Many have ideas of careers they would find interesting but are afraid they are not good enough or would not like the job. They delay making this choice by diving into video games or electronics, or by picking an unrealistic career such as YouTube Star or eSports athlete.

Fear often fuels their addiction to electronics, as they are uncertain about what they want for the future. Low self-esteem and social anxiety are often present, complicating the situation. For many, when they begin to combat their fear and take steps towards their future, their dependence on electronics decreases.

For your child, what role does fear have to play in their addiction? Could fear of people, or fear of the future be causing them to obsess with electronics? Also, what Needs are missing, that are driving this fear. Refer to Day 10 – 11 for the Chapter on Needs. For your child, finding the reason behind their addiction will serve to eliminate it.

Overwhelming Possibilities

Your child's generation is unique in the history of humankind. This is the first generation raised in the Internet Age. No other generation has had this much exposure to technology. As a result, your child's view of the world is vastly different than yours.

They see a world with thousands of career possibilities, each one full of challenges and competition. In some ways, this is good, as they do not fear electronics and hunger for them. However, many are afraid they will enter into a career they will dislike or not be good enough to succeed. They look at their parents as models and have determined they do not want to work 8-10 hours a day for an employer they do not like. Some refuse to accept the traditional model of work and have decided to do what they love: play video games or excel on social media. Many choose to become Bloggers, eSports Athletes, or YouTube Stars, not understanding the difficulty and amount of work it takes to succeed.

Your child may be overwhelmed by the number of careers available or may decide they take too much work or time. For your child to succeed, they need to begin thinking of realistic careers, ones they can achieve based on their talents.

Today's Activity

Today, you are going to meet with your child and begin discussing their career goals. During this discussion, listen to their ideas, and do not shoot them down. Even if they are unrealistic, you want to listen and ask how they will become successful.

If your child has an unrealistic goal, such as becoming an eSports Athlete, do not shut them down. Your goal is for them to conclude it is unrealistic, then look into alternatives. To do so, ask questions about how they will achieve this goal, and the amount of time and work it will take.

No matter the career goal, ask your child to begin researching it. You can help in the process, but you do not want to do all the work for them. Hopefully, they will start to see how realistic or unrealistic their goal is and what it takes to achieve it. Over time, discuss concerns you have over accomplishing this goal while considering alternative careers if their first choice does not work out.

Each month, you want to talk to your child about their career goals and what they have done to learn more about them. You can make activities out of this by scheduling trips or talks with people in these careers, so your child can see a real-world point of view. For now on, you need to speak to your child about their future and what they are doing to prepare.

Quick To-Do List

1. Conduct a meeting with your child about their career goals. Ask questions about their goals, and encourage them to research to learn more about them.

Tomorrow's Focus

While tomorrow ends your journey in this book, your child's struggle with addiction will continue. For now on, you will use what you have learned in this book as a framework for your family. Tomorrow, you will reflect on what you have learned about yourself, your child, and your family. This reflection will help you going forward as you continue to repair your family.

DAY 30: WHAT YOU HAVE LEARNED

Y ou did it; you reached the end of this book. If you followed the instructions in this book, much has changed with your family. Hopefully, some of it has been successful, while others have likely been difficult. It is time to reflect on what you have learned in this short period and how you can apply it to the future.

Personal Reflection

During this process, what did you learn about yourself? Were you able to control your emotions when things went wrong? Did you complete all the activities in this book? Did you follow the contract for yourself? Was this experience easier or harder than you imagined? Are you working to reframe ANTS, and if so, how has it changed you?

While this book has been about finding ways to combat your child's electronics addiction, in reality, it has been about changing you. From the beginning, my goal in this book has been for you to learn more about your child, their addiction, and how you fit into it. Your child cannot change unless you also change. As the adult and their parent, the focus is on you.

If this book has been a challenge, or if it did not turn out well, be honest. Some of the activities in this book will fail for your family. There is no shame or blame in this. Sometimes, our best plans fail.

For the future, what do you want to change in yourself? Beyond your child or family, what goals do you have for the future? These are important questions you need to answer. For each of the questions in this section, I want you to answer them for yourself. You do not need to show the answers to anyone.

- Did you complete all the activities in this book? If not, what challenges did you face to prevent you from doing so?
- During the last few weeks, did you use the coping skills in this book? If so, which one is your favorite, or works best for you?
- How did your child respond to the activities in this book?
- Were you able to control your emotions while placing limits on your child's screen time?
- Have you been working to reframe ANTS during the last part of this book? If so, what ANT occurs the most?
- Have you taken care of your health while working in this book?
- Has your child's sleep improved after removing electronics from their room?
- How has your family responded to the Contract? Are they following most of it? Did you make any changes to it on Day 28?
- Are you still monitoring your child's screen time, or was it too much to keep up with?
- Were you able to lock down your child's electronics? How did other family members respond?
- How has your spouse or partner, if any, reacted to the changes you have implemented with this book?
- How did your Family Days go? Do your children have any suggestions for improving them?
- Are you journaling every night? If so, how do you feel after?
- How do you see your family interacting one month from now, six months from now, and a year from now?
- What personal goals do you have for the future?

If you can think of any more questions you would like to answer, include them, as the above list are suggestions. Every few months, complete this list again to see what has changed with you and your family.

Tomorrow's Focus

I suggest starting over with this book and focus on the tasks you did not complete or the ones you found difficult. If it takes you ten tries to finish this book, it will be worth it. Understand, your child's addiction to electronics will continue, and will take some time to resolve. There is no quick, easy fix.

Focus on your health and your interactions with your child and your family. Your primary goal from now on is to improve the communication within your family. By making your family stronger, the addiction will become weaker. If you are seeing a therapist, for your child, your family, or yourself, continue. If not, find a therapist that is understanding, empathic, and willing to work with you and your family.

Last but not least, take a breath and relax. Completing this book was not an easy task. Take a moment to feel good about yourself, regardless of the outcome. By reading this book and completing the activities, you have decided to make a change. Continue this change by communicating with your family, making adjustments to the Contract, and spending more time together. Do something fun today, as your work continues tomorrow.

I want to thank you for reading this book. If you have comments, thoughts, or suggestions, please feel free to visit my website at https://nathandriskell.com. I plan to revise this book at least every two years. If there is something you would like added, let me know! If you have any specific questions, you can e-mail me, and I will promptly answer them. If you are in the Houston / Cypress area, I specialize in treating Internet Addiction in all forms, including gaming, social media, gambling, and pornography. I also provide Teletherapy services for the state of Texas, meaning I can see you online via webcam for therapy. Good luck, and be confident in yourself and your future!

RESOURCES

Logbook: Hours Spent Online

To download the logbook, follow the link below:

Logbook Link: https://nathandriskell.com/child-addicted-electronics/ online-hours-logbook-child-addicted-electronics.xlsx

Note: The logbook is an Excel file with tabs for each day you work in this book. You can copy tabs and make new days if you wish to expand on it.

Automatic Negative Thoughts (ANTS)

If you wish to learn more about Automatic Negative Thoughts (ANTS), please visit the website of Dr. Daniel G. Amen, M.D. He came up with the concept of ANTS and has resources that can help you learn to manage your thoughts better. To visit his website, follow the link below:

Dr. Daniel G. Amen: https://danielamenmd.com/

Needs List

The Needs list provided on Days 10-11 was created by the Center for Nonviolent Communication:

© 2005 by Center for Nonviolent Communication
   Website: www.cnvc.org E-Mail: cnvc@cnvc.org
   Phone: +1.505-244-4041

Online Meditation Channels

Below is a list of services that provide meditation channels. Most are free but come with advertisements, which you can remove if you subscribe to a monthly plan. Try the different channels and determine what works for you:

- Pandora: Online music service. Search for Meditation and try the different channels: http://www.pandora.com/
- Spotify: Online music service. Search for Meditation or Guided Meditation channels. https://www.spotify.com/·
- YouTube: Video playing service. Search for Guided Meditation or Meditation music. https://www.youtube.com/

Parental Control Software

Below is a list of the most used parental control software on the market today. I suggest checking each one out to determine if they will work on your devices and meet your needs. Parental control software is important for monitoring your child's online activities, as well as keeping them safe.

- **Norton Family Premier Link**: https://us.norton.com/norton-family-premier

- **Phone Sheriff Link**: http://www.phonesheriff.com/
- **ESET Parental Control For Android Link**: https://play.google.com/store/apps/details?id=com.eset.parental&hl=en
- **Net Nanny Link**: https://www.netnanny.com/
- **Qustodio Link**: https://www.qustodio.com/en/

About the Author

Nathan Driskell, MA LPC, is a therapist in the Houston, Texas area specializing in treating High Functioning Autism and Internet-related addictions. Nathan, who is on the Autism Spectrum, built a private practice to help people on the Autism Spectrum and who are addicted to electronics. Nathan is also a public speaker and has spoken at over 100 events throughout North America. Nathan works with children, teens, adults, and individuals who are addicted to electronics.

You can connect with me on:
- https://nathandriskell.com
- https://twitter.com/NathanDriskell
- https://www.facebook.com/nathandriskelltherapy

Also by Nathan Driskell

INTERNET ADDICTION: KICKING THE HABIT

Internet Addiction is a real and severe **addiction**. It can rob you of your **career**, **relationships**, and **life**. Ask yourself this: do you spend most of your time online? Would you rather spend time playing games than spending it with family and friends? Do you become anxious without access to your smartphone or computer? If so, you may have a problem. It is time to take back your life and live with a purpose! Internet Addiction: Kicking the Habit is available on Amazon via E-Book and Paperback.

Link: https://www.amazon.com/dp/B01LYD5MQ9

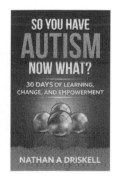

So You Have Autism, Now What?

Have you been diagnosed with Autism and feel lost, unsure what to do next? Do you find the world a strange and difficult place where it is hard to make friends and communicate with others? Do you find it difficult to go to school or begin a career due to your obsessions? It is time to learn who you are as a person and how to combat your Autism symptoms. Autism does not have to define you! So You Have Autism, Now What? is available on Amazon via E-Book and Paperback.

Link: https://www.amazon.com/dp/B08DCJXCJ8

Made in the USA
Las Vegas, NV
27 February 2023

68238738R00088